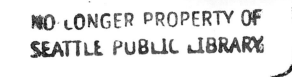

Sweet SUGAR Sultry SPICE

Sweet SUGAR Sultry SPICE

EXOTIC FLAVORS
TO WAKE UP YOUR BAKING

Malika Ameen

Roost Books

BOULDER

2016

Roost Books
An imprint of Shambhala Publications, Inc.
4720 Walnut Street
Boulder, Colorado 80301
roostbooks.com

First Edition
Printed in the United States of America

⊗ This edition is printed on acid-free paper that
meets the American National Standards Institute
Z39.48 Standard.
♻ Shambhala Publications makes every effort to
print on recycled paper. For more information
please visit www.shambhala.com.

Distributed in the United States by Penguin Random
House LLC and in Canada by Random House of
Canada Ltd

Book and cover design by Shubhani Sarkar

Library of Congress Cataloging-in-Publication Data

Names: Ameen, Malika.
Title: Sweet sugar, sultry spice: exotic flavors to wake
up your baking/Malika Ameen.
Description: First edition. | Boulder, Colorado: Roost
Books, [2016] | Includes index.
Identifiers: LCCN 2015030080 | ISBN
9781611802627 (hardcover: acid-free paper)
Subjects: LCSH: Desserts. | LCGFT: Cookbooks.
Classification: LCC TX773 .A375 2016 | DDC
641.86–dc23 LC record available at http://lccn
.loc.gov/2015030080

FOR YOU

Our loving Z

Keeper of my most precious.
Thank you for all that you do
and for all that you are.
We are lost without you.

Contents

Foreword

ASK MALIKA ABOUT OUR FIRST MEETING, and she will tell you a lovely story of simple hospitality and how a chef greeted her in the City of Angels. This much is certainly true, but my recollection runs much deeper.

It was a warm summer night in Los Angeles in 2003. Spago Beverly Hills was in full gear, humming with its perpetual energy. All the seats were filled and waiters commanded the floor, anticipating each guest's every need. The roar of the kitchen sounded in the distance as hundreds of plates rolled out from that well-oiled machine. As I worked in the pastry kitchen, I was informed via yellow sticky note: "There is a fellow chef at table 15. Can you stop by?"

At table 15, I saw an exotically beautiful woman with a smile that lit up the room. Her eyes sparkled with enthusiasm. Introductions complete, she asked for permission to inquire about the ingredients in the dessert she had just tasted.

I watched as she pursed her lips, pressed her tongue to the roof of her mouth, and closed her eyes to recall the flavors. After a moment, she recited a whirlwind of ingredients: "The sauce . . . strawberry sauce . . . it is much more than that. Are there raspberries in it? The spice is star anise, yet richer. Did you toast it first? And I get a hint of orange, but not just

orange . . . a bright, deep mandarin!" She went on next to the Kaiserschmarren, my signature soufflé. With a curious, coquettish smile, she asked about the nuances: "Crème fraîche? Rum? Ooohh, fromage blanc?"

She was a passionate sleuth, effortlessly discovering my recipe. I laughed and confirmed she had sussed out every one of my secrets. At that moment I knew I had met a new friend and a kindred spirit. Over the years we have shared countless meals together, from eighteen-course dinners to the perfect doughnut. Like recipe detectives, the name of the game is not to miss a single ingredient.

Malika is a rare breed of chef, skilled in both savory and sweet. She is a master of blending sugar and spice, and in *Sweet Sugar, Sultry Spice* she opens the door to her unique style of baking. You can taste her love for life and spice in every dessert, and we are fortunate that she has given us this gift: a trove of visionary recipes made with simple techniques and flavorful spices, from aniseed to za'atar.

Today, professional chefs and home cooks alike have access to an incredible array of the world's spices. Working with all those spices can be overwhelming—but not with Malika as your guide. She will teach you how to smell and taste spices and to use them to coax complex flavors from even the simplest ingredients. Your spice rack will become your new tool to transform your baking into something entirely different and magical.

In this wonderful book, Malika challenges us to think bigger—a morning muffin springs to life with fluffy ricotta, orange zest, orange blossom water, and currants, with aniseeds adding a whisper of licorice flavor (page 61). She expands our global horizons and takes us on culinary journeys with recipes such as the bright, fresh blueberry sumac handpies (page 129) and her delicious pomegranate milk chocolate scones with dried rose petals and rose water (page 103).

If I can share one piece of advice: dive into each recipe and discover Malika's secrets to creating flavor and adding spice to all you do. Thanks to her, the future of baking is rich, inspired, and full of spice.

SHERRY YARD
Chef-Owner, Helms Bakery

A Life of Spice

IF I WERE A SPICE, I WOULD BE CARDAMOM. It is the queen of spices, well rounded and complex with so many wonderful attributes. It's sweet, floral, and bright, with a whisper of citrus. It's bold but not overwhelming. It's everything you long for in a spice. And, for me, it is love. In Pakistan, where my parents come from, cardamom is used in everything from chai to *kulfi*, a sweet milk frozen custard, and people chew on cardamom pods as a breath freshener. Even now, when I catch the scent of the spice, I think of my mother, my *amma*. That scent takes me back to when I was growing up. I loved to watch Amma getting ready for a special evening out with my father, my *abbu*. She would gently fold the long pleats of her sari, one by one, the gold threads of the silk glimmering in the light. She would carefully place a few cardamom pods in the tiny side pocket of her silk-lined, beaded purse. Her gentle, loving kisses were fragrant with the aroma of the spice. For me, it will always be the comforting smell of home.

My earliest memories are cherished ones with my family. When I was growing up, my amma and abbu cooked together. They complemented each other perfectly in the kitchen. Watching them prepare a meal was like watching a couple waltzing, every step in perfect time and each movement gracefully choreographed. They would choose which dishes to cook, and then they would divide up the tasks, working side by side. They entertained at our house in suburban Chicago often, making elaborate Pakistani feasts. The delicious aromas would waft through the house, and long before the meal, the smell of spices would draw everyone to the kitchen. Even when it was just the four of us—my parents, my sister, and me—we always sat down to dinner together, at 6:30 sharp. It didn't matter what else we had going on. Everything came to a halt. It was time to eat, relax, and talk— to slow down and rejoice in being together. It was the part of my day I looked forward to the most.

Memorable family meals continued long after my sister and I had grown up and moved out. Saturday lunches became the ritual when my parents became grandparents; my sister and I have eight children between us. On Saturdays, my abbu, in his beige handcrafted Belgian linen apron, would cook recipes he had learned from his mother and his elderly great aunts. It was a big undertaking. Sometimes, Abbu would be on the phone as he cooked, consulting with his great aunt in London to make sure he got the recipes just right, jotting down notes on proportions and tips on methods. He would approach the meal much as I would in a restaurant creating a mise en place, with his knife sharpened, all his vegetables chopped, and his spices set out before he began to cook for our family. We were all his sous chefs.

At the time I owned a restaurant in Chicago, and Saturdays became a challenging time for a get-together. By Saturday afternoon, I should have been in the restaurant kitchen, preparing for a hectic night of service. But Abbu was cooking—we had to be there. I always had to hurry through lunch, leaving before everyone else finished to get back to the restaurant, but those meals were something that I looked forward to all week. They were therapeutic, an excuse to exchange stories and laugh together. I wasn't going to miss it. I yearned for that time with my parents, my sister, my nieces and nephews, and my sons all gathered around our family table together. My sons were very young, but I wanted them to experience the family meals that my parents so lovingly prepared.

I hope my boys appreciate that someday. I know I didn't always value it. As a child, I wanted anything other than Pakistani food. Every school day, when I opened my tin lunch box, the scent of coriander, cumin, chile, and cilantro instantly filled the air. Inside there was freshly squeezed juice and a sandwich with homemade *chapli kebab*, a spiced meat patty. I spent my prelunch hours daydreaming about juice boxes and all-American crustless peanut butter sandwiches.

I grew up surrounded by spice. It had absorbed into my skin and my soul—but I didn't want it to define who I was or where I was heading. I knew there was a whole world of culture and flavors to be explored.

YOU MIGHT NOT EXPECT IT OF A PAKISTANI girl growing up in Illinois in the early '80s, but traditional European pastry was a big part of my childhood. My amma was always trying out new recipes, and it was common in our house to follow our meal of spiced braised lamb and steaming, buttered basmati rice with a decadent dessert straight from a Julia Child cookbook. Abbu had a fondness for French pastries, and Amma aimed to please. I became obsessed with Martha Stewart's *Entertaining* in my early teens; I read through the trove of recipes carefully, bookmarking my favorites and planning what I would bake next. I tackled those recipes one by one, inviting friends and family over to relish in my latest creation. And, most important, there was Michel.

From the time I was seven years old, I had a weekend routine with my abbu. Every Saturday morning, we'd run errands in town and stop at the local gourmet market for cheeses. They had a pastry counter there, but we would pass right by. We were heading to Michel's Patisserie in the next town.

I remember everything about those trips to Michel's. I would walk past the window filled with decorated pastries and open the clear glass door. A little bell would go off and Michel would come running. He was exactly what you might imagine when you think of a European pastry chef, with a thick, groomed moustache and a delightful French accent. He was dressed all in white; he even had white clogs. He always greeted us with a boisterous "Bonjour!" his arms wide open for an embrace. He wanted to know how we were. How was school? And which of his irresistible sweets would we like to try today?

I was always so thrilled to be at Michel's. The bakery felt as welcoming as Michel was. The air was permeated with the smell of rich milky butter, sweet sugar, and freshly baked bread. I can still hear the gentle *jush-jush* of the glossy white European bread slicer. I remember the glass cases filled with French cookies,

fluffy petite meringues, sables, giant palmiers, and, of course, the sweet glazed smiley-face cookies Michel made, with colored sprinkles for hair and a big chocolate grin. I remember the refrigerator cases, too, with the tempting black forest cakes, silky chocolate mousse cakes, and colorful whipped cream fruit cakes glistening under the light.

Abbu always bought cinnamon raisin bread, which he would toast crisp and smear with a thin layer of butter to accompany his morning cup of tea. I loved the onion bread—a brioche with sautéed onions and leeks, topped with poppy seeds, as an after-school snack. My sister's first choice was the strawberry tart. I liked it, too. I would pick off all the plump, fresh berries, leaving the shortbread crust and the custardy vanilla cream filling dripping with strawberry juice for last. Oh, and the Florentines—buttery and nutty, with one side dipped in chocolate and the other decorated with those classic swirled ridges. I would devour the whole box on the ride home. It was only a short trip, but there would be nothing left but chocolate fingerprints on the little white and blue box, to my sister's immense disappointment.

Michel closed his shop when I was in my early teens, and we lost touch with him. Although I didn't think about those trips much as I got older, they were my first introduction to French pastry, which would be influential in my cooking career. Michel's was also where I first came to understand the bond that near-strangers could form over food.

I COOKED FOR MANY YEARS IN RESTAURANT kitchens, traveling from the East Coast to the West before returning to my hometown of Chicago to open my own restaurant. In time, I realized that as much as I loved the fast pace and creativity of working in restaurants,

I was ready for a new direction in my journey of food. But before I moved forward, I looked back through my desserts, and all the twists and turns of my cooking career. As I flipped through hundreds of recipes, I noticed something I didn't expect: spices, everywhere.

Almost every recipe used spices. They weren't always loud spices. They didn't make a fuss, but they were there, adding a whisper of flavor and aroma. I hadn't abandoned my traditional pastry training. Instead, without being aware of it, I had married the comforting flavors of my childhood and thousands of family dinners to the French pastries I had always loved and the pastry techniques I had learned in cooking school and honed in restaurants.

Spices have long been used in savory foods to enhance flavor and create complex and beguiling new tastes. This book will show you they do the same in sweet foods. There is an unending magic in spices, a power to change the way we experience flavors, to turn a familiar dessert into something entirely new. The spices were what made the desserts I created distinctive to me and special to the people I shared them with.

My perspective on individual spices was transforming, too. When I thought of cumin, now I wasn't only imagining my amma's biryani, that traditional Pakistani dish of slow-cooked rice layered with caramelized onions and spiced braised meat. Cumin—a spice I am so familiar with I can taste it in my mind—has so many sides to its personality I hadn't considered before. Spices can be warm or bright or floral or mysterious; some spices can be all those things. Spices are alluring, surprising, adventurous, comforting, or quiet.

The moment I realized I wanted all of those things in my food, as well as in my life, this book became my next project and my fixation. It further combines the flavors of

my childhood and of my family with my culinary training and experience in the food world—now I know I don't have to choose one over the other. Just as spices transform cooking, they have transformed me; when I cook with spices, I realize my true identity. This book is my spice story. I'm sharing it with you because spices will change your cooking journey, filling it with a wealth of exotic tastes and constant surprise. Through these spices you can unlock new worlds of flavor.

As fate would have it, while I was writing this book, two chef friends of mine traveled to France to spend the summer visiting their mentor. The man was reminiscing about the patisserie he once owned near Chicago and a kind man and his daughters who visited the shop every Saturday morning. As my friends listened, they slowly began to realize that he

was talking about my family. To my surprise and great joy, it was Michel! After twenty years, we were reunited. It was a momentous and crucial day for me, and the timing was without question magical. Tears streamed down my face as I revisited those precious memories tying me back to who I am. My life had come full circle, back to my hometown Chicago, to my love of French pastry, and to my passion for spices. Michel reminded me of how much food has meant in my life. Food connects people—family, friends, and even strangers. Food is our common ground. Over food we laugh, we cry, we share, and we create important memories that last our lifetime. Spices are the catalyst that make that all the more extraordinary, making memories more vivid and gratifying. I encourage you to dive into the world of spice, and unleash the endless possibilities.

Baking with Spices

WHAT IS A SPICE? THAT'S A SURPRISINGLY complicated question. In this book I think of a spice as any flavor enhancer that can—with just a pinch or a teaspoon—transform your cooking and awaken the senses to an unexpected world of possibilities. There's a whole universe beyond cinnamon and nutmeg. Berries, bark, seeds, leaves, and flowers—even extracts, essential oils, and minerals—can all be spices by my definition. They are inexpensive and versatile ingredients that bring excitement and sensuality to your food, and to the cooking process. For me, spices are a way to make food unique and memorable.

Spices tend to be an afterthought. We buy them at holiday time and they sit in our cabinets until the following year. But you can add spark to your meals every day by just reaching into the pantry. It isn't hard to introduce spices into your own cooking. Start slowly, smelling and tasting your spices before you add them to a recipe, to begin to understand the nuances of their aroma and flavor. And if you can't smell or taste anything, it's time to replace your spices. If you are cooking with spices that came from your grandmother's pantry, you'll never know how sensual spices can be. Freshness is essential.

When I think about spices, I'm thinking not just about the flavor of a spice but also the ways that spice can enhance or change other ingredients. I'm thinking about how the spices make me feel. That's what cooking is all about. The themes of the chapters in this book reflect that. Bakers like things to be precise, but these aren't strict, scientific categories. Spices are incredibly versatile, so I've divided recipes by the feelings and sensations spices evoke in them: Spicy and Warm; Floral and Aromatic; Bright and Fresh; Savory, Earthy, and Nutty; and Complex and Mysterious. You'll see some spices appear in multiple chapters, where they show off completely different sides of their personalities. In each recipe, I've highlighted the spice that I'm most excited about in the dessert. It might play a starring role or it might play a supporting role, but the dessert wouldn't be the same without it. If you want to learn more about any of the spices that appear in the recipes, turn to the glossary at the end of the book.

It's amazing how many things work well with sugar. Some of the spices featured in this book are very familiar to bakers and dessert lovers, but others are spices you've only ever tasted in savory dishes or have never even heard of at all. You just need to think about things a little bit differently. Forget what you know about a spice, and think about how you experience it. What does it taste like? What does it smell like? What does it remind you of? There's only one rule when baking with spices:

you can go crazy with your ideas, but you need to use restraint in executing them. Spice doesn't have to shout and overwhelm. Sometimes, a spice can tempt with just a whisper. As it turns out, the best approach to good cooking and eating is the same as the best approach to good living. You need to strike the right balance.

IN YOUR PANTRY

The desserts in this book were developed with many easy-to-find ingredients. When a recipe calls for a less common ingredient, I promise it's worth the effort to seek it out.

Sweeteners

Granulated sugar: The most common sugar. It can be purchased either refined (white) or natural. I like to use the natural because it is unbleached and richer in flavor. It has a slightly brown tinge from the molasses in the sugarcane. All recipes in this book will work with either kind.

Sanding sugar: A coarse, large-grained sugar that is often dyed and used for decorating baked goods. Sanding sugar does not melt in the oven when heated.

Turbinado sugar: Made from the initial pressing of sugarcane, with natural molasses remaining in the sugar crystals. I love its rough texture, which can create a crunchy finish when sprinkled on desserts before baking.

Brown sugar: White granulated sugar with molasses added back in to deepen its color and flavor. It comes in "light" and "dark" varieties, with the dark having a more pronounced molasses flavor, and it must be packed firmly before measuring.

Muscovado sugar: A minimally processed, unrefined cane sugar from which the molasses has not been removed. It is usually labeled "light" (with less molasses) or "dark." Muscovado sugar is much darker and richer in flavor

than brown sugar, with a fruity, earthy aroma. Its texture is moist and sticky. Equal amounts of light or dark brown sugar can be substituted for muscovado sugar.

Molasses: A thick and sweet dark syrup. Molasses is a by-product of processing sugarcane into sugar. It lends a robust and distinctive tangy flavor to baked goods. All recipes in this book are made with unsulphured molasses, which should not to be confused with blackstrap molasses, which is stronger in flavor.

Honey: The well-known sweetener produced by bees. There are endless varieties available, ranging from mild to robust. All recipes in this book are best with a mild honey like flowery clover, woodsy linden, or fruity orange blossom honey unless otherwise noted. Good-quality honeys are available at farmers' markets and better supermarkets.

Maple syrup: The boiled sap of the sugar maple tree. Use pure—not imitation—maple syrup. It comes in several versions: Grade A and Grade B are the most widely recognized. All the recipes in this book were made with Grade B, which has a more intense flavor that is great for baking. Grade A is a fine substitute.

Maple sugar: A granulated-style sugar with a rich and smooth maple flavor. Maple sugar is produced by boiling the sap of the sugar maple tree past the point of maple syrup until all the water has evaporated. It is about twice as sweet as regular granulated sugar.

Coconut palm sugar: An unrefined, nutrient-rich sugar that adds a warm color and a deep caramel flavor to baking. This brown-colored sugar is produced by tapping the sweet nectar from the tropical coconut palm tree and drying the juice in a large open kettle.

Date sugar: Finely chopped dry dates. Date sugar lends a subtle creamy texture and a mild flavor reminiscent of dates.

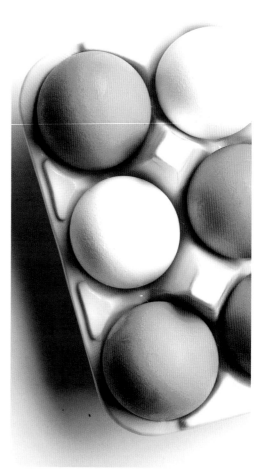

Flours

It is critically important to measure flour correctly when baking. Many recipes don't turn out right because of this simple mistake. To measure flour, always stir flour in the bag or in a container first to aerate it. Dip the measuring cup into the flour and gently sweep the cup to fill it without compressing the flour. Level the flour with a knife.

Unbleached all-purpose flour: The most common flour used in baking. I always use unbleached flour, as bleached flour has added chemicals and harmful additives. These recipes were tested with King Arthur flour, which is milled with a mixture of hard and soft wheats.

Cake flour: Finely milled flour with a lower protein content than all-purpose flour. It produces tender cakes and pastries.

Whole wheat flour: A wheat flour that also includes both the germ and the bran, which give it a robust flavor. It has a higher oil and fiber content and should be kept tightly wrapped and refrigerated to prevent it from going rancid. I love it for its nutty, down-to-earth flavor. A little bit of whole wheat flour substituted for all-purpose flour can raise a baked good to elegant heights.

Oat flour: A nutty, toasty flour with all the flavor of oats without the texture. It is simply oats milled to a fine flour. It adds not only good flavor but also lightness and delicate texture to baked goods. Store it in an airtight container in the freezer for up to six months.

Buckwheat flour: A dark, flavorful flour made by roasting buckwheat seeds and then milling them to a fine powder. Its flavor is assertive, earthy, and strong. Store it in an airtight container in the freezer for up to six months.

Fine semolina (also known as sooji): Soft wheat ground to a sandy texture. (Not to be confused with the more yellow-colored semolina made from hard durum wheat.) Pale-colored fine semolina gives a nutty, sweet flavor to desserts. You can always substitute a little bit of semolina for all-purpose flour to add texture to your baked goods. Fine semolina is available at many Asian and Middle Eastern grocers. Cream of Wheat is a good substitute. Store semolina in an airtight container at room temperature for up to three months or in the freezer for up to six months.

Nut flours: Made from finely ground nuts. Nut flours add a wonderful flavor as well as a soft texture to baked goods because they are free of gluten. All the recipes in this book were made with natural almond flour, but blanched is a fine substitute, as they are interchangeable. Store them in an airtight container in the freezer for up to six months.

Tapioca flour: A thickener derived from cassava root. A few recipes in this book call for tapioca flour—also called tapioca starch—to thicken desserts. I like tapioca flour more than cornstarch in certain recipes because it doesn't have a starchy aftertaste. You can substitute cornstarch in equal proportion, but remember that cornstarch needs a higher heat to thicken. Quick-cooking granulated tapioca is also used to thicken desserts, but it is processed differently and works differently in a recipe; don't confuse one with the other.

Butter and Oils

Unsalted butter: The most common baking fat. High-fat, unsalted European-style butter is my choice for baking. Its higher milk fat and lower water content mean a fuller flavor and beautiful browning. If European-style butter is too expensive, a good-quality, unsalted grade A butter will work just fine. You can always splurge on the recipes in which butter is a key ingredient, such as shortbread, pie crusts, or galette dough. Always buy unsalted butter so you can control the amount of salt in your recipe.

Coconut oil: A great baking fat yielding rich and moist results. The flavor and texture complement many baked goods and impart a subtle coconut flavor. You can substitute coconut oil in any recipe in this book that calls for grapeseed oil or olive oil. Coconut oil can also be substituted one-to-one in place of butter.

Grapeseed oil: Pressed from the seeds of grapes. Grapeseed is my go-to oil for baked goods because of its neutral flavor and lightness. You can substitute vegetable oil if you wish.

Olive oil: A great oil for baking, imparting a subtle peppery flavor and richness to desserts. For most of these desserts, you'll want to use a mild, cooking-grade olive oil for a noticeable but understated effect. But for the Roasted Grape Focaccia (page 149), choose a high-quality, fruity extra-virgin olive oil. Its flavor will shine.

Peanut oil: Best for frying. Its flavor is milder than canola or vegetable oil, and it produces crispy, less greasy fried desserts.

Chocolate

Dutch-process cocoa powder: All recipes in this book call for Dutch-process cocoa, also known as European style. The cocoa is treated with an alkali solution that neutralizes the acids present in the cocoa, which reduces bitterness. Dutch-process cocoa powder is not the same as natural cocoa powder, which is lighter in color and has a much higher acidity.

Chocolate: Many recipes in this book call for chocolate, be it unsweetened, milk, bittersweet (also called dark), or white. Buy the best quality chocolate possible because it will give the best results. It should have a smooth mouthfeel and a rich flavor. For the recipes that call for bittersweet chocolate, I used one with 60 to 64 percent cocoa content.

Salt

I always use kosher salt in my baking—probably because I worked in restaurants for most of my career, where it is the salt of choice. Its coarse grains allow you to control the amount you are using, and it has a milder, cleaner flavor than table salt. (You cannot substitute different salts in a one-to-one ratio because their grains are different sizes.) Salt is extremely important in baking, as it pulls forth the true flavors of baked goods.

ON YOUR SPICE RACK

Buying good-quality spices and storing them well may be one of the most important secrets to successfully baking with spices.

Buying Spices

Good-quality, pure, and unadulterated spices are becoming increasingly available. Your best vendor options are either a grocery store that does a brisk business selling spices by weight or a local spice shop, where you can start a conversation with a spice expert and learn lots

about the spices on offer. If you are looking for a hard-to-find spice, there are also many trusted mail-order sources. (See the Resources section for some of my favorites.)

When buying spices, you are looking for freshness. If you can, get your nose into the spice container and smell it. You'll know instantly if it's a good choice. A spice's volatile oils, which provide its aroma and much of its flavor, can dissipate quickly, muting the spice or changing its character. For that reason, it's best to buy whole spices when they are available and to grind them yourself. That's not a hard task, and it also allows you to control the texture of the spice. It's also best to buy only as much of the spice as you will use in a short period of time. Spices don't age well on their own—they bloom and age beautifully in baked goods. Some recipes in this book call specifically for freshly ground or grated spices. The recipes were tested with freshly ground and preground spices.

Some spices, namely the herbs and flowers I include in this category, are available both fresh and dried. Both versions have their place in the kitchen, but they are not interchangeable. They have different flavors and different textures, and the strength of their flavor in particular can be very different. Substitute a dried spice for a fresh one, and the dessert might be overwhelmed by the spice. For spices available in both versions, I've noted which one should be used in the recipe. One other note: when baking with flowers—fresh or dried—always buy food-grade flowers. You don't want to be eating a chemically treated bouquet or bit of potpourri.

Some of the recipes in this book call for extracts. You won't get the same powerful flavor from the whole spice itself. When baking with a new brand of extract, start with a little less of the extract than the recipe calls for and taste it before adding more.

Storing Spices

One easy and economical way to store spices is in baby food jars. The jars are small and airtight, slowing the evaporation of essential oils and preventing the spices from picking up off flavors. My point is, you don't need to get fancy about storing your spices: any airtight container placed in a cool spot away from direct sunlight will work. If necessary, you can also store whole spices in an airtight container in the freezer for up to three months. There are many options available in the retail market for storing spices.

If you buy whole spices, store them that way, grinding only as much as you need for a specific recipe.

Preparing Spices

There are some basic tools and techniques that make it easy to bake with spices.

TOOLS

Coffee grinder: An electric coffee grinder allows you to quickly grind small amounts of spice into a fine powder. Be sure to clean it thoroughly with a damp paper towel after each use so that one spice doesn't contaminate the next. To give the grinder a more thorough cleaning, grind dried bread, empty the grinder, and then clean with a damp paper towel. The bread will capture any leftover spices.

Mortar and pestle: Grinding spices by hand with a clay, marble, or wooden mortar and pestle gives you greater control over the texture of your spices. It is especially useful in achieving the coarse ground texture that is key to some recipes.

Microplane zester/grater: This simple kitchen tool is invaluable for grating whole nutmeg and cinnamon sticks as well as citrus zest. It is indispensable.

TECHNIQUES

Texture: When baking with spices, the texture of the spice is often important. How a spice is prepared can affect both the flavor and mouthfeel of the baked good. Crushing a spice, for instance, will release different flavors than finely grinding it. And a coarsely ground spice will provide a texture that a finely ground one won't. I've provided directions in the recipes where this is important.

Toasting: Toasting can intensify the fragrance and taste of a spice and change its flavor and appearance. Spices should be toasted in a dry pan over medium heat until fragrant. I've provided specific instructions in the recipes.

Steeping: Some spices—particularly teas and flowers—are steeped in hot liquid to release their flavors. Be careful not to steep the spices for longer than the recipe calls for. The results can be bitter or overpowering. It's important to set a timer to remind yourself when to strain the steeping liquid.

*T*HERE'S NOTHING MORE COMFORT-ing and inviting than the warm and spicy smell of cinnamon filling the house when you are baking. It evokes loving memories of family and friends gathering together. It always reminds me of apple pie, one of Amma's favorite desserts. But cinnamon and the other fall favorites, nutmeg and ginger, aren't the only spices that can create that coziness. Clove, mace, allspice, and even bay leaf can feel like a welcoming warm embrace. And peppercorns and chiles stoke the flame further, bringing a sweet heat to your desserts.

Spicy AND Warm

Four-Spice Ginger Cookies

ACTIVE TIME: 20 minutes
TOTAL TIME: 2 hours, 30 minutes

Makes 3 dozen cookies

1 cup all-purpose flour

1 teaspoon baking soda

½ teaspoon kosher salt

½ teaspoon ground Vietnamese cinnamon

¼ teaspoon ground ginger

1 teaspoon ground cardamom

¼ teaspoon freshly ground white peppercorns

¼ teaspoon Dutch-process cocoa powder

1 cup granulated sugar, divided

2 tablespoons firmly packed light brown sugar

2 teaspoons finely grated orange zest

5 tablespoons (2½ ounces) unsalted butter, melted then cooled to room temperature

White from 1 large egg

1½ teaspoons peeled and grated fresh ginger

2 tablespoons unsulphured molasses

½ teaspoon vanilla extract

I'm obsessed with ginger cookies because of my amma's adoration of gingersnaps. I've spent years trying to create the perfect ginger cookie for her. To give this chewy version its complex flavor, I use more than just the ginger. The secret is white pepper, a surprising ingredient that gives the cookies more warmth than ginger alone. Plus there's cardamom for floral sweetness and fresh orange zest for a pop of brightness. A writer at the *Chicago Sun Times* once told me these were the best ginger cookies she's ever had. But, more important, my amma loves them. Whenever I bake these for her, a handful disappear from the tray, added to the secret stash she keeps in the freezer for whenever a craving hits her.

IN A MEDIUM BOWL, WHISK TOGETHER THE FLOUR, baking soda, salt, cinnamon, ground ginger, cardamom, white pepper, and cocoa. In the bowl of a standing mixer, combine ¾ cup of the granulated sugar and the brown sugar and orange zest. Gently rub the mixture between your fingers to release the oils in the zest. Add the butter and beat on medium speed until combined. Add the egg white, fresh ginger, molasses, and vanilla and beat until smooth. Add the flour mixture and beat on low until combined. Transfer the dough to the refrigerator and chill 2 hours or overnight.

Preheat the oven to 350°F. Line a baking tray with parchment paper. Put the remaining ¼ cup of the granulated sugar in a shallow bowl. Scoop out 1 teaspoon of dough and roll it between your hands to make a ball. Roll the ball in the sugar to coat. Place on the prepared baking tray and repeat with the remaining dough. (If dough begins to get warm and soft, chill it for 5 to 7 minutes, until it firms up.) Bake for 8 to 10 minutes for chewy cookies or a little bit longer for crispier ones.

MAKE AHEAD: The dough can be stored in the refrigerator for up to 1 week or in the freezer for up to 1 month. Defrost dough before using.

STORE: The cookies can be stored at room temperature in an airtight container for up to 5 days.

This cake reminds me of cotton candy—with a fiery kick. The angel food cake has a soft and fluffy texture, and when it's baking, your house will smell like a carnival. Then there's the glaze: it's bright red from the tart dried raspberries and has the fruity, smoky undertones and biting spice of chipotles. Chipotles are dried, smoked jalapeños. They are bold and hot, and their flavor gets stronger as the glaze sits, so don't be fooled by the small amount called for in the recipe.

Angel Food Cake

PLACE THE EGG WHITES IN THE BOWL OF A STAND MIXER fitted with a whisk attachment. Allow to stand until the egg whites reach room temperature, 30 to 45 minutes, depending on the temperature of your kitchen. Position an oven rack in the lower third of the oven. Preheat the oven to 350°F. Locate a 10-inch tube pan. Sift the flour, confectioners' sugar, and salt onto a sheet of parchment paper. Return the flour mixture to the sieve or sifter and repeat two more times.

Whip the egg whites in the mixer until frothy. Add the cream of tartar and whip on medium speed until foamy. With the mixer running, gradually add the granulated sugar and whisk until soft peaks form. (Be careful not to overwhip to the point of stiff peaks, or the cake will collapse when baking.) Add the vanilla and fold in with a spatula to incorporate. Sprinkle one quarter of the flour mixture over the whites. Using the rubber spatula, fold the flour into the whites. Repeat with the remaining flour mixture, folding in a quarter of the mixture at a time. With a large spoon, carefully transfer the mixture into the ungreased tube pan.

(Continued)

Angel Food Cake with Raspberry–Chipotle Glaze

ACTIVE TIME: 20 minutes
TOTAL TIME: 2 hours

Serves 12 to 14

ANGEL FOOD CAKE

1½ cups egg whites, from about 12 cold large eggs (see Note)

1 cup cake flour, sifted

1½ cups confectioners' sugar

¼ teaspoon kosher salt

1½ teaspoons cream of tartar

1 cup granulated sugar

1 teaspoon vanilla extract

1 cup fresh raspberries, for garnish

RASPBERRY-CHIPOTLE GLAZE

1¾ cups confectioners' sugar, sifted

¼ cup finely ground freeze-dried raspberries

Scant ¼ teaspoon ground chipotle

Scant ¼ teaspoon kosher salt

½ teaspoon vanilla extract

5 to 6 tablespoons freshly squeezed lemon juice

SPECIAL EQUIPMENT

10-inch tube pan

NOTE: Cold eggs separate more easily than warm eggs.

MAKE AHEAD: You can make the angel food cake 1 day in advance and store it, tightly wrapped, at room temperature. Glaze the cake the day you plan to serve it.

Bake for 40 to 45 minutes, until the cake is lightly golden, it springs back when touched, and a wooden toothpick inserted into the center comes out clean. Invert the cake pan onto a cooling rack. Let it cool completely before removing from the pan. To remove the cake, slip the tip of a metal spatula between the cake and the pan. Slowly work the tip around the perimeter to release any cake sticking to the pan. Tilt the pan on its side and gently tap it against the countertop to loosen the cake. Cover the open end of the pan with a cooling rack, invert the pan onto the rack, and tap the pan firmly to release the cake onto the rack. Allow to cool completely.

Raspberry–Chipotle Glaze

IN A MEDIUM BOWL, WHISK TOGETHER THE CONFECTIONers' sugar, ground raspberries, chipotle, and salt. Add the vanilla and 5 tablespoons lemon juice and whisk until smooth. The consistency should be thin enough to be easily pourable but still thick enough to spread. Add more lemon juice as appropriate to achieve the desired consistency.

To put it all together

TRANSFER THE COOLED CAKE ONTO A PLATE. POUR THE glaze over the top of the cake and, with an offset spatula, quickly smooth the glaze so it drizzles evenly down the sides of the cake and there's a nice even coating on the cake top. Let the cake sit for at least 1 hour to allow the glaze to set. Garnish the cake with fresh raspberries before serving.

The smell of honey baking in the oven is one of the kitchen's most tempting aromas. Here, I use an amber honey to take pineapple upside-down cake to a whole new level. Amber honey is more distinctive than everyday mild honey but not as overwhelming as dark honeys. That means you get a honeyed crust that doesn't overpower the moist, allspice-y cake packed with caramelized pineapple. (Hint: This is best with a ripe pineapple. Buy one that's not too green on the outside and has a sweet, heady fragrance. Don't be afraid to pick it up and smell it right there in the produce department.)

Pineapple Squares

PREHEAT THE OVEN TO 325°F. SET ASIDE 2 TABLESPOONS of the butter. Lightly grease an 8-inch square pan with just enough butter to help parchment paper adhere to the pan. Line the pan with 2 criss-crossed pieces of parchment, creating a 1-inch overhang. Coat the parchment paper generously with the remaining butter. Sprinkle the bottom of the pan with 3 tablespoons of the turbinado sugar.

Trim, peel, and core the pineapple and cut the fruit into ½-inch cubes. You should have about 3 cups of fruit. Line a small baking tray or plate with paper towels. Arrange the pineapple cubes on the towels and pat the cubes with additional paper towels to remove as much surface liquid as possible. Set a 10- to 12-inch heavy-bottomed skillet over high heat for 3 minutes. (A cast iron pan works great here.)

Transfer half the pineapple pieces to a medium bowl and toss with 3 tablespoons of the granulated sugar and a pinch of salt. Drop 1 tablespoon of the butter into the preheated skillet. Once the butter melts and begins to sizzle, add the sugared pineapple and distribute over the pan in a single layer, making sure that each piece lies flat. Once the bottoms are brown, use tongs or a fork to carefully turn each cube onto another side. If the sugar begins to get too dark, lower the heat to medium. Continue to brown all sides of the pineapple cubes, a process that will take 6 to 7 minutes. Transfer the browned pineapple to a separate bowl. Wipe the pan

(Continued)

Luscious Pineapple and Honey Squares

ACTIVE TIME: 45 minutes
TOTAL TIME: 1 hour, 30 minutes

Makes 16 squares

PINEAPPLE SQUARES

4 tablespoons (2 ounces) unsalted butter, divided

¼ cup turbinado sugar, divided

1 small ripe pineapple

½ cup plus 2 tablespoons granulated sugar, divided

½ teaspoon kosher salt, plus 2 pinches

1¼ cups all-purpose flour

¾ teaspoon baking powder

1 teaspoon ground Vietnamese cinnamon

¼ teaspoon ground cloves

¾ teaspoon freshly ground allspice

¼ cup hot, strong coffee, or ¼ cup hot water combined with 1¼ teaspoons espresso powder

¾ cup amber honey or Caramelized Honey (see recipe that follows)

2 large eggs, at room temperature

½ cup grapeseed or other neutral oil

½ teaspoon vanilla extract

CARAMELIZED HONEY

¾ cup mild honey

clean with a paper towel and return to high heat. Toss the remaining pineapple with 3 tablespoons of the granulated sugar and a pinch of salt. Drop the remaining 1 tablespoon butter into the pan and repeat the process of browning the pineapple pieces. Transfer the browned pineapple to the bowl with the other cooked pineapple. There should be about 1 tablespoon of pineapple juice remaining in the pan when you are done. (If there's more than 1 tablespoon, continue to cook until the liquid reduces.) Reserve the juice for the cake.

In a medium bowl, sift together the flour, baking powder, and remaining ½ teaspoon kosher salt. In another medium bowl, stir together the cinnamon, cloves, and allspice with the hot coffee (this brings out the flavor of the spices). Add the amber honey to the coffee mixture and whisk to combine. (If using hot caramelized honey, allow the coffee mixture to cool to room temperature after adding the honey.) In a large bowl, whisk together the eggs, oil, remaining ¼ cup granulated sugar, and vanilla. Add the coffee mixture to the egg mixture and whisk to combine. Add the flour mixture to the egg mixture and gently whisk until free of lumps. Fold in the pineapple pieces and reserved juice. Pour the batter into the prepared pan and sprinkle with the remaining 1 tablespoon of turbinado sugar.

Bake for 30 minutes, turn the pan, and bake an additional 40 to 45 minutes, until a wooden toothpick inserted into the center comes out clean. Let cool completely. Invert the cake to remove it from the pan and cut into 16 squares.

Caramelized Honey

PUT THE HONEY INTO A HEAVY-BOTTOMED SAUCEPAN over high heat and cook, stirring occasionally. It will bubble furiously. It is done when the honey is fragrant and the bubbles are a light amber color, 5 to 6 minutes. (If you cook it longer, it will harden and be difficult to incorporate into the cake batter.) Add the hot honey to the recipe immediately.

STORE: This cake will keep for up to 3 days in the refrigerator.

SPICY AND WARM

"Almond Joy" Crunch

ACTIVE TIME: 10 minutes
TOTAL TIME: 35 minutes

Makes 4 cups

CRUNCH

1 vanilla bean

¼ cup plus 2 tablespoons
granulated sugar

½ cup water

2 medium-sized dried bay leaves

2½ cups unsweetened coconut chips
(not sweetened shredded coconut)

½ cup sliced almonds with skin

3 tablespoons raw cocoa nibs

2 heaping tablespoons
Candied Orange Zest
(see the recipe that follows),
store-bought candied orange
(see page 252), or
1¼ teaspoon finely grated orange zest

¼ cup turbinado sugar

1 teaspoon fleur de sel

CANDIED ORANGE ZEST

4 navel oranges

3 cups water, plus additional water
for blanching

4 cups granulated sugar

2 tablespoons
freshly squeezed lemon juice

When I worked in restaurants, my abbu would always ask when I was going to put a coconut dessert on the menu. They were his favorite, and he would happily be a taste tester for all my ideas. He would have loved this crunchy confection. It reminds me of the Almond Joy candy bar so many of us grew up with—but with a sophisticated twist of spice and candied orange. The vanilla bean plays well with the coconut, and bay leaves give perfume, spice, and a very subtle peppery kick. Little salty hits of fleur de sel come into play every few bites. And, of course, the cocoa nibs give you the experience of pure, unadulterated chocolate. With a little sweet, a little salt, a little chocolate, and a lot of crunch, this is my go-to during a late-night TV binge. It makes a wonderful snack, a topping for ice cream or yogurt, or a great hostess gift packed in a little bag with a ribbon.

Crunch

PREHEAT THE OVEN TO 350°F. LINE A BAKING TRAY WITH a nonstick baking mat or greased parchment paper.

Slice the vanilla bean lengthwise and scrape out the seeds. In a small saucepan over high heat, combine the vanilla bean pod and seeds and the granulated sugar, water, and bay leaves and bring to a boil. Stir, then lower the heat to medium and simmer until liquid is reduced to ⅓ cup, about 5 minutes.

In a large bowl, stir together the coconut chips, almonds, and cocoa nibs. Add the ⅓ cup sugar syrup (including the bay leaves and vanilla pod) and the candied orange zest and stir. In a small bowl, whisk together the turbinado sugar and fleur de sel. Sprinkle the sugar-salt mixture over the coconut mixture and stir well. Spread the mixture evenly on the prepared baking tray. Bake, stirring every 7 to 10 minutes, for about 20 to 22 minutes, until golden brown. Allow to cool. (I store the crunch with the bay and vanilla bean still in it. You won't want to eat them, but they look pretty and continue to lend their fragrance.)

(Continued)

MAKE AHEAD: The candied orange zest can be made ahead and stored in the refrigerator for up to 1 month.

STORE: "Almond Joy" Crunch can be stored in an airtight container at room temperature for up to 1 week.

Candied Orange Zest

CUT OFF THE ENDS OF THE ORANGES AND CAREFULLY score the orange peel from end to end into 5 segments, cutting through the pith but not into the fruit. Carefully remove the strips of orange peel, leaving the flesh intact.

Fill a medium saucepan with cold water and add the orange peels. Bring the water to a boil and cook the orange peels for 5 minutes. Drain. Follow this process twice more to reduce the bitter flavor of the pith.

Once the peels have been boiled 3 times, lay them on a cutting board and allow to sit until cool enough to handle, about 5 minutes. With a spoon, gently scrape off most of the white pith, leaving about ⅛ inch remaining. Cut the orange peels lengthwise into ¼-inch strips.

Combine the sugar, 3 cups water, and lemon juice in a medium saucepan over medium-low heat. Bring to a simmer. Add the strips of orange peel and cover the pan. Simmer until the orange zest is translucent and soft, about 1½ hours.

This decadent cake has all the flavors of warm and spicy Mexican-style hot chocolate. The rich, moist devil's food cake is spiced with just enough cayenne pepper to tickle the tongue. And the deep, rich chocolate ganache is perfumed with the floral notes of Ceylon cinnamon. Freshly ground Ceylon cinnamon makes this cake all the more special and flavorful, but you can use preground instead. I toast the marshmallow frosting with a blowtorch for a playful finishing touch.

Devil's Food Cake

PREHEAT THE OVEN TO 350°F. GREASE TWO 8-INCH round pans, then line each with a circle of parchment paper cut to fit into the bottom.

Sift together the flour, sugar, cocoa powder, baking soda, baking powder, salt, cinnamon, and cayenne into the bowl of a stand mixer fitted with a paddle attachment. In a medium bowl, whisk together the buttermilk, oil, eggs, and vanilla. With the mixer on low speed, slowly add the buttermilk mixture to the flour mixture, beating until just combined. In a small bowl, stir together the hot water and espresso powder. With the mixer on low speed, slowly add the espresso mixture to the batter. The finished batter will be very thin.

Divide the batter evenly between the prepared pans. Bake for 30 to 35 minutes, until a wooden toothpick inserted into the center comes out clean. Let the cakes cool in their pans for 20 minutes, then run a knife around the edges of the pans to loosen the cakes and invert them onto a cooling rack.

Cinnamon Ganache

WHILE THE CAKES ARE BAKING, PREPARE THE CINNAMON ganache. In a small saucepan over medium-high heat, combine the cream and cinnamon. Bring to a boil, then immediately remove from the heat, cover, and let steep for 1 hour. Strain the spiced cream through a fine-mesh sieve over a medium bowl. Discard the cinnamon. Return the spiced cream to the saucepan, stir in the espresso powder, and bring to a simmer over medium-high heat.

(Continued)

Mexican Hot Chocolate Cake

ACTIVE TIME: 45 minutes
TOTAL TIME: 3 hours, 30 minutes

Serves 12

DEVIL'S FOOD CAKE

1¾ cups all-purpose flour

2 cups granulated sugar

¾ cup Dutch-process cocoa powder

2 teaspoons baking soda

1 teaspoon baking powder

1 teaspoon kosher salt

1½ teaspoons freshly ground Ceylon cinnamon

1 teaspoon ground cayenne

1 cup buttermilk

½ cup grapeseed oil

2 large eggs, at room temperature

1 teaspoon vanilla extract

1 cup hot water

1 tablespoon espresso powder, or 1 cup strong brewed coffee

(Continued)

SPICY AND WARM

Put the chocolate, corn syrup, butter, and salt into a medium bowl. Pour the simmering cream over the mixture and let stand for 2 minutes, allowing the heat from the cream to melt the chocolate. Whisk until smooth. Cover the ganache with plastic wrap pressed to its surface and let stand until cool and thick, about 2 hours.

To assemble the layers

PLACE A COOLED CAKE LAYER IN THE CENTER OF A PLATE. Measure ½ cup of the cooled ganache into a small bowl and set aside. Spread the remaining ganache evenly over the first cake layer. (The ganache layer will be about ½ inch thick.) Place the second cake layer on top of the filling, then spread the reserved ½ cup ganache evenly over the top of the cake. Refrigerate the cake for about 20 minutes, or until the ganache has hardened. (Use this time to make the marshmallow frosting.)

Marshmallow Frosting

FILL A LARGE SAUCEPAN WITH WATER A QUARTER TO one-third full, and bring to a boil over high heat. Reduce the heat to maintain a gentle simmer. Combine the egg whites, sugar, cream of tartar, water, and corn syrup in the bowl of a stand mixer. Rest the mixer bowl over the saucepan of gently simmering water and whisk frequently until the sugar has dissolved and the syrup is warm to the touch. Fit the stand mixer with a whisk attachment and whip the syrup on medium speed until billowy marshmallow fluff forms, 3 to 4 minutes. Add the vanilla and salt and whip for a few seconds until incorporated. Use immediately.

To put it all together

FROSTING THE CAKE: AFTER THE GANACHE HAS HARDened, remove the cake from the refrigerator and use a rubber spatula to spread the marshmallow frosting over the top. Use the tip of the spatula to create lots of swoops and swooshes. Using a blowtorch, toast the marshmallow frosting until the peaks are golden brown.

MAKE AHEAD: The cinnamon ganache can be made in advance and stored in the refrigerator. Remove from refrigerator 1 hour before using.

CINNAMON GANACHE

2 cups heavy cream

One 7-inch Ceylon cinnamon stick, broken into pieces

2 teaspoons espresso powder

1 pound bittersweet chocolate, roughly chopped

1 tablespoon light corn syrup

2 tablespoons (1 ounce) unsalted butter, at room temperature

Scant ¼ teaspoon kosher salt

MARSHMALLOW FROSTING

Whites from 2 large eggs

⅔ cup granulated sugar

Pinch of cream of tartar

1 tablespoon water

⅓ cup light corn syrup

1 teaspoon vanilla extract

Pinch of kosher salt

SPECIAL EQUIPMENT

Blowtorch (optional)

NOTE: Ceylon cinnamon tends to come in varying widths. For this recipe, I used a fat stick that was 1 inch thick. Thinner sticks tend to be about half as thick. You can adjust accordingly, adding a little more if you have thinner pieces of cinnamon.

SPICY AND WARM

Sticky Roasted Rhubarb

ACTIVE TIME: 10 minutes
TOTAL TIME: 30 minutes

Serves 4 to 6

1 teaspoon tapioca flour

1 teaspoon cold water

½ cup firmly packed light brown sugar

½ cup mild honey

4 star anise pods

1 tablespoon plus 1 teaspoon peeled and grated fresh ginger

1 teaspoon kosher salt

1 teaspoon unsalted butter

¼ teaspoon orange oil, or 1 tablespoon finely grated orange zest

1 pound rhubarb, cut diagonally into 2-inch pieces

This enticing, viscid syrup is great drizzled on ice cream, served with cake, or swirled into your morning oatmeal. It's so good you'll want to savor every last drop. The tart rhubarb is balanced by the earthy brown sugar and honey. The orange oil gives freshness, the ginger gives a little spicy tingle at the back of your throat, and the star anise is a whisper of licorice in the background. It's a sweet, tart, and simple take on a favorite springtime ingredient.

PREHEAT THE OVEN TO 350°F.

In a small bowl, whisk together the tapioca flour and cold water to make a smooth paste. In a small saucepan over medium heat, combine the tapioca paste, brown sugar, honey, star anise, and ginger. Bring to a boil and simmer for 5 minutes. Remove from the heat and whisk in the salt, butter, and orange oil.

Put the rhubarb in a roasting pan, pour the sauce over it, and toss to coat. Bake for 7 to 15 minutes, until the rhubarb is just fork tender (you don't want it to become mushy). Baking time will depend on the thickness of the stalks. Remove the rhubarb pieces from the hot liquid and space apart on a separate tray or plate to cool down somewhat so they don't overcook in the sauce. Strain the sauce, removing and discarding spices. Recombine the rhubarb and sauce and serve warm.

STORE: Allow the rhubarb and sauce to cool completely and transfer to an airtight container. Store in the refrigerator for up to 1 week. To serve, warm up the sauce and then add the rhubarb.

Ooh, those Little Debbie Creme Pies. I can still remember biting through the soft, chewy cookies and into the sugary white frosting. I just had to pay homage to this favorite childhood treat. In this grown-up rendition, black pepper, brown butter, and honey are waiting for you in the cream filling sandwiched between two oatmeal-spice cookies. As I assemble these, I can't keep my fingers out of the frosting. I didn't think I'd have to share these cookies with my kids—I was sure the spark of black pepper would scare them off—but they ate the entire first batch.

Chewy Oatmeal Cream Pies

ACTIVE TIME: 35 minutes
TOTAL TIME: 1 hour

Makes 24 cream pies

Oatmeal Cookies

PREHEAT THE OVEN TO 325°F. TOAST THE PECANS ON A baking tray until dark brown and fragrant, about 10 minutes. Once the pecans have cooled, roughly chop. Turn the oven up to 350°F. Line two baking trays with nonstick baking mats or parchment paper.

In a food processor, combine ¾ cup of the oats with the dried apples. Process until the oats are finely ground and the apple pieces are no larger than ¼ inch. In a medium bowl, whisk together the ground oats and apples, the remaining ½ cup of oats, and the pecans, flour, baking powder, baking soda, salt, ginger, cinnamon, and mace until incorporated.

In the bowl of a stand mixer fitted with a paddle attachment, beat the butter, oil, sugar, molasses, and agave. Beat on medium speed until light and fluffy, 3 to 4 minutes. Add the egg and beat until incorporated. Add the oat and flour mixture all at once and beat on low speed until combined. Add the milk and beat well, scraping down the sides of the bowl with a rubber spatula as needed.

Use a tablespoon to drop dollops of dough onto the prepared baking trays, 12 cookies to a tray. Bake 8 to 9 minutes, until the cookies have puffed and colored slightly. The centers of the cookies may appear to be underdone, but they will firm up as they cool. Allow to cool completely on the pan.

(Continued)

OATMEAL COOKIES

½ cup pecan halves

1¼ cups thick rolled oats, divided

½ cup roughly chopped dried apples

1¾ cups all-purpose flour, divided

½ teaspoon baking powder

1½ teaspoons baking soda

¾ teaspoon kosher salt

Heaping ¼ teaspoon ground ginger

Heaping ¼ teaspoon ground Vietnamese cinnamon

⅛ teaspoon ground mace

8 tablespoons (4 ounces) unsalted butter, at room temperature

¼ cup coconut oil, or grapeseed oil

1 cup granulated sugar

2 tablespoons unsulphured molasses

¼ cup plus 2 tablespoons agave syrup

1 large egg, at room temperature

¼ cup whole milk

(Continued)

BLACK PEPPER CREAM FILLING

12 tablespoons (6 ounces) unsalted butter, at room temperature, divided

1¾ cups confectioners' sugar, sifted

1 tablespoon mild honey

2 tablespoons heavy cream

1 teaspoon vanilla extract

¼ teaspoon kosher salt

1¾ teaspoons freshly ground black pepper

Black Pepper Cream Filling

IN A SMALL SAUCEPAN OVER MEDIUM-HIGH HEAT, MELT 4 tablespoons of the butter and cook, stirring frequently, until brown and nutty, 2 to 3 minutes. Transfer the browned butter to a small bowl, being sure to scrape all the brown bits. Chill in the freezer until cold and firm.

In the bowl of a stand mixer fitted with a paddle attachment, beat together the chilled brown butter, the remaining 8 tablespoons of room-temperature butter, and the confectioners' sugar on medium speed until creamy. Add the honey, cream, vanilla, salt, and black pepper and beat well.

To put it all together

ONCE THE COOKIES HAVE COOLED, SPOON A SCANT 1 tablespoon of black pepper cream filling onto the bottom of a cookie. Top with an unfilled cookie to make a sandwich with the cream filling in the center. Repeat with the remaining cookies and filling.

MAKE AHEAD: You can make the dough in advance and refrigerate it or freeze it. The frosting can be stored in a separate airtight container in the refrigerator for up to 3 days. Allow both to come to room temperature, then beat briefly in a stand mixer before using.

STORE: These cookies can be stored in an airtight container at room temperature for up to 3 days.

This smoothie is a little dessert in a glass. It's also a great part of a brunch spread or an afternoon pick-me-up for you or your kids. It comes together with the push of a button, and you can personalize it, too. You can add a little honey or agave for a sweeter smoothie (although I think the dates make it perfectly sweet), cocoa powder for a chocolate treat, or a banana for something more filling. In every variation, the almond milk gives the smoothie a satisfying custard-like texture, and the nutmeg not only rounds out the flavors but also offers a surprising finish that makes this smoothie sing in your mouth.

PLACE THE DATES IN A SMALL BOWL AND COVER WITH boiling water. Let stand until very soft, about 5 minutes. Drain, pushing out any excess water. Slice the vanilla bean lengthwise and scrape out the seeds. Discard the pods or set aside for another use. Put the soaked dates, vanilla bean seeds, almond milk, cinnamon, and nutmeg into a blender and puree until smooth. Add the crushed ice and blend again. Serve immediately.

MAKE AHEAD: The smoothie base can be made without the ice and stored in the refrigerator for up to 2 days. To serve, just add ice and blend.

Creamy Date and Almond Smoothie

ACTIVE TIME: 8 minutes

Serves 6

²/₃ cup firmly packed, pitted medjool dates

1 vanilla bean

2 cups unsweetened almond milk

½ teaspoon ground Vietnamese cinnamon

Pinch of freshly grated nutmeg

Ice

I just *had* to name these "lusty." They are so alluring. The Meyer lemons give the curd a sunshine yellow color that looks stunning on top of the dark chocolate crust. And they taste as sexy as they look: the lemon curd is floral and tart, and the chocolate crust is rich, with the delicate fruitiness and pop of pink peppercorns. (If you want to use conventional lemons instead of Meyer lemons, increase the sugar in the curd by ¼ cup. Conventional lemons are much tarter.)

Spiced Chocolate Crust

GREASE AN 8-INCH SQUARE PAN. LINE WITH 2 PIECES OF parchment paper, crisscrossed to create a 2-inch overhang on all sides.

Use a mortar and pestle to crush the pink peppercorns and partially grind them. (Don't leave any of them whole.) In the bowl of a stand mixer fitted with a paddle attachment, combine the crushed peppercorns, flour, confectioners' sugar, cocoa powder, salt, cinnamon, and cloves. Add the butter and beat on low speed until a smooth dough forms. Press the dough into the prepared pan, evenly coating the bottom and reaching ½ inch up the sides of the pan. (These sides are important: If the crust doesn't reach higher than the lemon filling, the filling will seep over the edges of the crust and leak under it during baking.) Freeze the dough until very firm, about 30 minutes.

Preheat the oven to 350°F. Grease a piece of parchment paper or a coffee filter and place over the chilled crust, coated side down. Fill the crust with pie weights (or uncooked rice or beans). Bake for 30 minutes, then remove from the oven and let stand for 10 minutes. Remove the weights and parchment. Continue baking the crust for another 15 minutes, or until firm to the touch. Allow to cool to room temperature.

(Continued)

Lusty Lemon Squares

ACTIVE TIME: 35 minutes
TOTAL TIME: 4 hours, 30 minutes

Makes 16 squares

SPICED CHOCOLATE CRUST

1½ teaspoons pink peppercorns

¾ cup all-purpose flour

¼ cup plus 2 tablespoons confectioners' sugar, sifted

3 tablespoons Dutch-process cocoa powder

½ teaspoon kosher salt

¼ teaspoon ground Vietnamese cinnamon

⅛ teaspoon ground cloves

8 tablespoons (4 ounces) unsalted butter, at room temperature

MEYER LEMON CURD

1 tablespoon finely grated Meyer lemon zest

¾ cup granulated sugar

4 large eggs plus the yolks of 2 large eggs

2 tablespoons heavy cream

1 cup freshly squeezed Meyer lemon juice

4 tablespoons (2 ounces) unsalted butter

¼ teaspoon kosher salt

½ teaspoon vanilla extract

1½ to 2 tablespoons confectioners' sugar, for garnish

Meyer Lemon Curd

PUT THE LEMON ZEST AND SUGAR INTO A MEDIUM BOWL and rub the mixture between your fingers to release the oils in the zest. Add the eggs, egg yolks, and cream, and whisk until incorporated.

In a medium saucepan, stir together the lemon juice and butter and bring to a simmer over medium heat. Once simmering, slowly add the lemon juice mixture to the egg mixture, whisking continuously to incorporate. Return the mixture to the saucepan and cook over medium-low heat, whisking continuously, until the mixture thickens into curd and lightly coats the back of a spoon, about 5 minutes. Strain the curd through a fine sieve into a medium bowl. Stir in the salt and vanilla. Cover with plastic wrap pressed to the surface of the curd and let cool to room temperature.

To put it all together

PREHEAT THE OVEN TO 350°F. POUR THE STRAINED Meyer lemon curd into the baked chocolate crust and spread it evenly. Bake for 18 to 20 minutes, until the curd jiggles only slightly when shaken. Allow to cool to room temperature and then refrigerate until the filling is firm, 2 to 3 hours. (The longer it chills, the easier it will be to cut.)

Use the overhanging parchment paper to remove the chilled dessert from the pan to a cutting board. Using a long serrated knife, trim off all 4 edges. Cut the square in half and then in halves again to create 4 even strips. Cut each strip into 4 pieces to make 16 even squares. Lightly dust with the confectioners' sugar.

This is an ultra-moist, deluxe version of your grandma's carrot cake, with a heady zing of ginger. Fresh, ground, and candied ginger each play a unique and delicious role in the cake. I like my carrot cake fully loaded with chunks of walnuts, currants, and pineapple, but you can omit any of these to suit your tastes. I also piled on oat flour, which gives the cake a soft, moist crumb and a toasty flavor to balance the heat of the fresh ginger, and tahini, which is a delightful, nutty addition to the expected cream cheese glaze.

Triple Ginger Carrot Cake

ACTIVE TIME: 35 minutes
TOTAL TIME: 2 hours

Serves 12

Carrot Cake

PREHEAT THE OVEN TO 325°F. ON A BAKING TRAY, TOAST the walnuts for 5 minutes, stir, and bake for another 5 minutes. When cool enough to handle, roughly chop the walnuts.

Turn the oven up to 350°F. Generously butter and flour a 10-inch Bundt pan.

In a medium bowl, sift together the all-purpose flour, oat flour, baking powder, baking soda, salt, cinnamon, and ground ginger. In the bowl of a stand mixer fitted with a paddle attachment, beat the oil, granulated sugar, brown sugar, pineapple, eggs, vanilla, and grated ginger on medium speed until thoroughly combined, about 1 minute. Add the flour mixture and beat on low speed until incorporated, scraping down the sides of the bowl as needed. Add the carrots, currants, and chopped walnuts and beat on low speed to combine. Scrape down the sides with a rubber spatula and stir by hand to make sure everything is evenly distributed. Transfer to the prepared Bundt pan.

Bake for 45 to 50 minutes, until a wooden toothpick inserted into the center comes out clean, turning the pan halfway through to ensure even baking. Allow the cake to cool in the pan.

(Continued)

CARROT CAKE

1 cup walnut halves

1½ cups plus 2 tablespoons all-purpose flour

½ cup plus 2 tablespoons oat flour

2 teaspoons baking powder

1 teaspoon baking soda

1 teaspoon kosher salt

2 teaspoons ground Vietnamese cinnamon

1 tablespoon ground ginger

1 cup grapeseed oil

1 cup granulated sugar

1 cup firmly packed light brown sugar

One 8-ounce can crushed pineapple, drained

4 large eggs, at room temperature

2 teaspoons vanilla extract

3 tablespoons plus 1 teaspoon finely grated fresh ginger

3 cups shredded carrots

½ cup currants

2 tablespoons finely chopped candied ginger, for garnish

(Continued)

CREAM CHEESE GLAZE

4 ounces full fat cream cheese,
at room temperature

2 tablespoons (1 ounce) unsalted
butter, at room temperature

1¼ cups confectioners' sugar, sifted

1 teaspoon vanilla extract

1 tablespoon tahini

2 tablespoons whole milk

⅛ teaspoon kosher salt

Cream Cheese Glaze

IN THE BOWL OF A STAND MIXER FITTED WITH A PADDLE attachment, beat the cream cheese and butter on medium speed until smooth. Add the confectioners' sugar and beat until incorporated. Add the vanilla, tahini, milk, and salt and beat well to combine.

To put it all together

TURN OUT THE CARROT CAKE ONTO A PLATE. SPOON THE cream cheese glaze over the cake so that the glaze runs down the sides. Garnish with the candied ginger.

STORE: The cake can be covered and stored in the refrigerator for up to 2 days.

Grapefruit Jewels

ACTIVE TIME: 20 minutes
TOTAL TIME: 4 hours

Serves 4 to 6

1 teaspoon white peppercorns

½ teaspoon black peppercorns

¼ cup granulated sugar

1 teaspoon fresh thyme leaves

¼ cup water

⅛ teaspoon kosher salt

2 cups freshly squeezed
pink or red grapefruit juice

½ pink or red grapefruit, for garnish

Whipped cream, for garnish
(recipe on page 88)

When I was growing up, Sunday morning breakfasts included a pink grapefruit half sprinkled with salt and black pepper. I loved the combination. That pink grapefruit was a very American breakfast food—but the spices gave it an Asian flavor. In South Asia, it's very common to see fruit paired with savory spices. In this refined interpretation of our childhood breakfast, I use white pepper as well as black. White peppercorns are actually black peppercorns that have been soaked to remove the outer casings. This gives the white peppercorns a more intense flavor with a slightly fermented taste and smell.

USE A MORTAR AND PESTLE TO LIGHTLY CRUSH THE white and black peppercorns. In a small saucepan, combine the sugar, thyme leaves, and crushed peppercorns with the water. Bring to a boil over high heat, then reduce the heat and simmer until the liquid has reduced to 5 tablespoons. Strain the liquid through a fine-mesh sieve over a medium bowl and discard the solids. Stir the salt into the liquid and let cool. Add the grapefruit juice to the cooled syrup and stir well. Transfer the mixture to a 9 × 13-inch pan. Freeze for about 3 hours, using a fork to scrape and break up the surface every hour until the mixture is slushy. Peel the ½ grapefruit, divide into sections, and chop. To serve, spoon the granita into small bowls and top with grapefruit and whipped cream.

MAKE AHEAD: Store the granita, covered tightly, for up to 2 weeks in the freezer.

MAKE AHEAD: The dough can be made in advance and placed side by side on a baking tray, double layered with parchment paper in between. Refrigerate for up to 3 days or freeze for up to 1 month.

STORE: These cookies can be stored in an airtight container at room temperature for up to 2 days but are best eaten the day they are baked.

These rich, decadent cookies are a favorite of Martha Stewart's. She invited me to bake them on her show, and she loved them so much, she took the entire batch with her to serve at her holiday open house. When you taste them, you'll understand why. This dense cookie holds chunks of dark, milk, and white chocolate—it's like biting into a truffle—and there is a subtle trace of cinnamon as the chocolate melts on your tongue.

SIFT TOGETHER THE ALL-PURPOSE FLOUR, CAKE FLOUR, cinnamon, cocoa powder, baking powder, baking soda, cream of tartar, and salt into a medium bowl.

In the top of a double boiler over gently simmering water, combine 12 ounces of the bittersweet chocolate, the unsweetened chocolate, and the butter. Allow the chocolate to melt. Roughly chop the remaining 5 ounces of bittersweet chocolate, the white chocolate, and the milk chocolate and set aside.

In the bowl of a stand mixer fitted with a paddle attachment, beat together the warm chocolate, eggs, and egg yolks until just combined. Add the granulated sugar, vanilla, and coffee extract. Beat just until combined. Add the flour mixture and beat until just combined, scraping down the bowl as needed. Add chopped chocolate and mix on low speed until just incorporated. Cover the dough and refrigerate for 1 hour or overnight.

Preheat the oven to 325°F. Line two baking trays with nonstick baking mats.

Place the sanding sugar in a shallow dish. Fill a second shallow dish with water. Using a ¾-ounce ice cream scoop, scoop out the dough; press down on the tops of the dough with your thumb. Dip the bottom of each portion of dough in water, then in the sanding sugar; place them, equally spaced, on the prepared baking trays.

Bake for 7 to 8 minutes, until cookies are just set. The cookies will still look slightly wet, but they will firm up once cooled.

NOTE: If you don't have cake flour, all-purpose flour can be substituted.

Chocolate Truffle Cookies

ACTIVE TIME: 45 minutes
TOTAL TIME: 2 hours

Makes 6½ dozen cookies

⅓ cup all-purpose flour

2 tablespoons cake flour

1 teaspoon ground Vietnamese cinnamon

3 tablespoons Dutch-process cocoa powder

¼ teaspoon baking powder

¼ teaspoon baking soda

⅛ teaspoon cream of tartar

½ teaspoon kosher salt

17 ounces bittersweet chocolate, divided

4 ounces unsweetened chocolate

5 tablespoons (2½ ounces) unsalted butter

10 ounces white chocolate

5 ounces milk chocolate

3 large eggs plus the yolks from 3 large eggs, at room temperature

1⅓ cups plus 2 tablespoons granulated sugar

2¾ teaspoons vanilla extract

1⅛ teaspoons coffee extract, or 1 teaspoon espresso powder in 1 teaspoon hot water

1 cup coarse white sanding sugar

Crumbly Maple Walnut Penuche Bars

The most pungent of all spices, cloves are used sparingly to bring a profound complexity to dishes like this one. These bars have a gooey, fudge-like texture and a deep maple flavor similar to penuche fudge. Spicy cloves temper the sweetness of the maple sugar and dark maple syrup, giving the bars an inviting warmth that makes you want to take another bite. And another one. And another one. I particularly love these buttery treats with a cup of strong, piping hot coffee.

ACTIVE TIME: 20 minutes
TOTAL TIME: 1 hour, 30 minutes

Makes 18 diamonds

MAPLE SHORTBREAD

1¼ cups all-purpose flour

½ teaspoon kosher salt

1 teaspoon ground cloves

8 tablespoons (4 ounces) unsalted butter, at room temperature

¼ cup firmly packed light brown sugar

1 teaspoon pure Grade B maple syrup

WALNUT TOPPING

½ cup walnut halves

9 tablespoons (4½ ounces) unsalted butter, at room temperature

2 tablespoons pure Grade B maple syrup

½ cup maple sugar

½ teaspoon kosher salt

2 tablespoons light corn syrup

¼ cup heavy cream

Maple Shortbread

BUTTER AN 8-INCH SQUARE PAN. LINE WITH A PIECE OF parchment paper large enough to create a 2-inch overhang on two sides. Butter the lining but leave the overhang unbuttered.

Whisk together the flour, salt, and cloves in a medium bowl. In the bowl of a stand mixer fitted with a paddle attachment, beat the butter and brown sugar. Beat on medium speed until the mixture is pale and fluffy, 2 to 3 minutes. Add the flour mixture and maple syrup and beat on low speed until well combined, stopping periodically to scrape down the sides of the bowl. Transfer the dough into the prepared pan and press into the bottom. Chill for at least 30 minutes and as long as overnight.

Preheat the oven to 350°F. Bake for 20 to 25 minutes, until shortbread is a pale golden color and set in the middle.

Walnut Topping

PREHEAT THE OVEN TO 325°F. TOAST THE WALNUTS ON A baking tray for 5 minutes, turn the tray, and bake for another 5 minutes. Set aside.

In a medium saucepan over medium-high heat, stir together the butter, maple syrup, maple sugar, salt, corn syrup, and cream. Bring to a boil. Boil, stirring constantly, for 3 minutes (setting a timer is helpful). Remove the pan from the heat and let stand for 2 minutes. Add the toasted walnuts and let it stand until cool enough to be spreadable but not runny, 3 to 5 minutes. (If it is too hot, it will pour down the sides of the crust.)

To put it all together

SPREAD THE WARM WALNUT TOPPING OVER THE SHORT-bread and let cool completely. (You can refrigerate for 15 minutes or up to 1 hour to speed up this process.) Lift the shortbread out of the pan using the parchment paper overhang. Using a sharp serrated knife, cut the shortbread square diagonally into 6 even sections, then turn 90 degrees and cut each section into 8 bars, yielding a total of 18 diamonds (plus some decadent scraps).

MAKE AHEAD: The plain short-bread can be frozen for up to 2 weeks. Warm the short-bread in a 300°F oven for 7 to 10 minutes before adding the walnut topping.

STORE: Store these bars in an airtight container at room temperature for up to 5 days. The bars will also keep well in the freezer for up to 2 weeks.

SPICY AND WARM

Lacey Oatmeal Cranberry Crisps

This sweet treat is both elegant and easy to put together. Warm, sharp, and bracing nutmeg is the star of this crunchy caramelized cookie. Its great flavor is underlined by a big dose of tangy orange zest. They make a great holiday treat, but I like them as an everyday teatime cookie, too.

PREHEAT THE OVEN TO 350°F. LINE A BAKING TRAY WITH parchment paper.

Slice the vanilla bean lengthwise and scrape out the seeds. Discard the pods or set aside for another use. Combine the seeds with the granulated sugar and gently rub the mixture between your fingers until the sugar looks slightly coarse. In a medium saucepan, stir together the brown sugar, granulated sugar with vanilla seeds (if using), orange zest, nutmeg, and salt. Add the butter and corn syrup. Set over medium-high heat and cook until the entire mixture starts to bubble, 3 to 4 minutes. Whisk until smooth. Add the oats, almonds, and cranberries and stir until well incorporated. Let stand to cool for 15 minutes.

Use a tablespoon to drop dollops of dough onto the prepared baking tray, leaving 3 inches between cookies. Press each piece of dough gently with the palm of your hand to flatten slightly. (This will help it spread evenly when baking.) Bake for 12 to 14 minutes, until golden brown and bubbly. Allow to cool for several minutes on the baking tray, then transfer to a cooling rack.

STORE: Store these cookies in an airtight container for up to 1 week.

ACTIVE TIME: 15 minutes
TOTAL TIME: 50 minutes

Makes 2 dozen cookies

1 vanilla bean

¼ cup granulated sugar

1 cup firmly packed dark brown sugar

1½ teaspoons finely grated orange zest

½ teaspoon freshly grated nutmeg

⅛ teaspoon kosher salt

5 tablespoons unsalted butter

¼ cup dark corn syrup

1½ cups thick rolled oats

½ cup sliced almonds with skin

½ cup dried cranberries, roughly chopped

Classic persimmon pudding is a favorite of mine, but it has two drawbacks: it is often too sweet, and with their short season, persimmons can be hard to find. Here, I used dried persimmons, which are always available and have a consistent and intense flavor, to make a less-sweet custard. After much trial and error, I realized the custard is even better as an ice cream, creamy and rich with the deep flavor of honey. When you add the whole wheat crumble to the ice cream, you get a cross between a cake and a pudding.

Honey Persimmon Ice Cream

IN A MEDIUM SAUCEPAN OVER MEDIUM-HIGH HEAT, combine the persimmon pieces, cinnamon sticks, and water. Bring to a boil. Boil for 5 minutes, then reduce the heat to low, cover the saucepan, and simmer until the persimmons have absorbed all the liquid and are fork tender. (If the persimmons are hydrated but still appear very wet, cook over low heat for another 1 to 2 minutes, stirring frequently, to dry them.) Discard the cinnamon sticks. You should have ⅔ cup persimmons, packed.

In a separate medium saucepan over medium-high heat, bring the honey to a boil and cook until it is lightly caramelized and fragrant, 4 to 5 minutes. Slowly add the heavy cream, milk, and salt, whisking to combine. Return the honey mixture to a boil. While the liquid is heating, whisk together the egg yolks, brown sugar, and vanilla in a medium bowl. When the honey mixture boils, slowly pour half the honey into the yolk mixture, whisking continuously. Pour the honey-yolk mixture into the saucepan with the remaining honey mixture and whisk to combine. Cook over medium-low heat, stirring constantly, until the custard mixture is thick enough to thinly coat the back of a spatula, 2 to 3 minutes.

(Continued)

Honey Persimmon Ice Cream with Brown Sugar Crumble

ACTIVE TIME: 30 minutes
TOTAL TIME: Overnight

Makes 1 quart

HONEY PERSIMMON ICE CREAM

4 ounces dried persimmons, broken into 1-inch pieces

Three 2½-inch cinnamon sticks

1½ cups water

½ cup mild honey

1½ cups heavy cream

1½ cups whole milk

½ teaspoon kosher salt

Yolks from 6 large eggs

¼ cup firmly packed light brown sugar

1 teaspoon vanilla extract

1½ teaspoons ground ginger

¼ teaspoon freshly ground allspice

(Continued)

¼ cup plus 2 tablespoons
whole wheat flour

¼ cup all-purpose flour

¼ cup firmly packed dark muscovado
or dark brown sugar

2 tablespoons granulated sugar

¾ teaspoon ground Vietnamese
cinnamon

⅛ teaspoon freshly grated nutmeg

¼ teaspoon kosher salt

5 tablespoons (2½ ounces)
unsalted butter, melted

Whipped cream, for garnish (optional)
(recipe on page 88)

SPECIAL EQUIPMENT

Ice cream maker

Put the stewed persimmon, ground ginger, allspice, and half of the custard mixture into a blender. Blend on medium speed until the texture is very smooth, about 2 minutes. Add the remaining vanilla custard and blend to incorporate. Strain the mixture through a fine-mesh sieve over a bowl, cover, and store in the refrigerator overnight.

Transfer the custard to an ice cream maker and process according to the manufacturer's instructions.

Brown Sugar Crumble

PREHEAT THE OVEN TO 350°F. LINE A BAKING TRAY WITH parchment paper.

In a medium bowl, whisk together the whole wheat flour, all-purpose flour, muscovado sugar, granulated sugar, cinnamon, nutmeg, and salt. Break up any lumps of sugar with your fingers. Add the melted butter and stir with a spatula until mixture sticks together in large clumps. Chill the crumble in the refrigerator until firm, about 10 minutes.

Sprinkle clumps of chilled crumble onto the prepared baking tray. Bake for 18 to 20 minutes, tossing with a spatula halfway through baking, until lightly browned. Let cool completely.

To put it all together

CHILL A LARGE METAL BOWL IN THE FREEZER FOR ABOUT 15 minutes, until icy to the touch. Transfer freshly churned ice cream into the bowl and gently fold in the cooled whole wheat crumble. Freeze for at least 2 hours, or until firm enough to scoop. Serve with soft whipped cream, if using.

STORE: Ice cream can be stored in an airtight container in the freezer for up to 2 weeks.

N BIG SUR, THE AIR SMELLS LIKE HERBS, SWEET WILDFLOWERS, salt, and burnt honey. The ocean disappears into the sky there, and the sunsets are so beautiful they stop all conversation. I have such fond memories of visiting that magical place with my eldest son—and it has inspired some of my favorite desserts. Floral or pungent, aromas are a powerful thing in baking, even more powerful than taste. Just think of how amazing your kitchen smells when you bake with spices like cardamom, saffron, and orange blossom water. Every time I bake with lavender, I am transported back to Big Sur by the flowers' heady fragrance. The magic of baking is that it can take you anywhere.

Floral AND Aromatic

Peach–Buttermilk Popsicles

ACTIVE TIME: 35 minutes
TOTAL TIME: 5 hours

 *Makes* 10 Popsicles

1 pound ripe yellow peaches (nectarines are also delicious, or a combination), quartered and pitted

1/3 cup plus 3 tablespoons granulated sugar, divided

1 cup heavy cream

3/4 teaspoon dried lavender buds

Yolks from 4 large eggs

1/2 teaspoon kosher salt

1 teaspoon vanilla extract

1 cup buttermilk

SPECIAL EQUIPMENT

Ice pop molds

This is a pastry chef's Popsicle. You start with a crème anglaise. It's not hard—and it gives the Popsicles a soft, creamy texture. The creamy lavender base and ripe, sweet peaches remind me of summer days strolling the L.A. farmers' markets. (If there's a little peach puree left over after you make the Popsicles, that's the chef's treat. It's marvelous in a smoothie or slathered on top of a warm piece of buttered toast.) Actually, I'm eating one of these Popsicles as I write this. All I have left to say is, this is utterly divine!

PREHEAT THE OVEN TO 425°F. LINE A 13 X 18-INCH baking tray with parchment or a nonstick baking mat.

In a medium-sized bowl toss the peaches with 3 tablespoons of the sugar and transfer to the baking tray. Roast for 7 to 11 minutes, depending on the ripeness of the peaches, until fork tender. Allow the peaches to cool on the pan, then peel off the skin and mash the flesh with a fork right on the pan or puree in a blender. Transfer the mixture to a bowl and chill in the refrigerator.

Combine the cream and 3 tablespoons of the sugar in a small saucepan and bring to a simmer. Stir in the lavender buds and turn off the heat. Steep for 10 minutes but no longer. (If you oversteep the lavender, the mixture will taste soapy.) Strain the mixture over a small bowl and discard the solids. Return the liquid to the saucepan and bring to a boil.

In a medium bowl whisk together the remaining 2 tablespoons plus 1 teaspoon of sugar, egg yolks, and salt. Temper the egg mixture by adding a few tablespoons of the hot cream mixture to the bowl while whisking vigorously. This will warm but not cook the eggs. Add the remaining hot cream mixture slowly, whisking continuously. Return all the liquid to the saucepan. Cook over low heat, stirring continuously, until the custard coats the back of a wooden spoon. Stir in the vanilla and buttermilk. Chill in the refrigerator, covered with plastic wrap, for 1 hour.

To make the Popsicles, fill each of 10 ice-pop molds with 1/2 tablespoon of the peach puree. Add the buttermilk custard until the molds are filled halfway. Top with another

½ tablespoon of the peach puree and then add more custard, leaving a ⅛-inch gap at the tops of the molds. Using a thin knife or wooden skewer, gently swirl the mixture in each mold. (Don't overmix—you want a marbled effect.) Insert the ice-pop sticks and freeze until solid, at least 4 hours.

MAKE AHEAD: These Popsicles are best made 1 or 2 days before serving so they have time to freeze well.

STORE: Store in the freezer for up to 2 weeks.

FLORAL AND AROMATIC

These muffins are Sunday morning muffins to be enjoyed over a leisurely cup of coffee. The ricotta creates a rich and fluffy crumb that's not too heavy, and the currants stud the muffins with little chewy bites. The muffins are fragrant with citrus and have a tickle of licorice from the toasted aniseed. Best served with a newspaper—and the time to read it.

PREHEAT THE OVEN TO 350°F. LINE ONE AND A HALF muffin pans with 18 paper liners.

In a skillet over medium heat, toast the aniseeds until fragrant, about 2 minutes. Use a mortar and pestle to crush the seeds. In a small bowl, use your fingers to combine the crushed aniseeds, ¾ cup of the sugar, and the orange zest and remove any clumps in the mixture. Set aside.

In a large bowl, combine the remaining ¾ cup of sugar and the flour, baking powder, baking soda, and salt. In a separate large bowl, whisk together the eggs, oil, butter, sour cream, ricotta, and orange blossom water. Pour the ricotta mixture over the flour mixture and gently fold in with a rubber spatula until just combined. The batter will be thick. Fold in the currants.

Scoop the batter into the prepared muffin cups, about ⅓ cup of batter per muffin. Top each with 1 heaping teaspoon aniseed sugar, patting the aniseed sugar down lightly so it will stick to the dough.

Bake for 18 to 20 minutes, until a wooden toothpick inserted into the center of a muffin comes out clean.

STORE: These muffins can be stored in an airtight container at room temperature for up to 2 days.

Fluffy Ricotta Muffins

ACTIVE TIME: 30 minutes
TOTAL TIME: 50 minutes

Makes 18 muffins

1 tablespoon aniseeds

1½ cups granulated sugar, divided

1 teaspoon finely grated orange zest

3 cups all-purpose flour

1 tablespoon baking powder

½ teaspoon baking soda

1 teaspoon kosher salt

4 large eggs

⅔ cup plus ¼ cup grapeseed oil

2 tablespoons (1 ounce) unsalted butter, melted

½ cup sour cream, at room temperature

1 cup whole milk ricotta, at room temperature

2 teaspoons orange blossom water

1 cup dried currants

Walnut Cardamom Snowballs

ACTIVE TIME: 40 minutes
TOTAL TIME: 2 hours

Makes 3 dozen cookies

16 tablespoons (2 sticks; 8 ounces) unsalted butter, at room temperature

½ cup granulated sugar

1½ teaspoons ground cardamom

1 teaspoon vanilla extract

¼ teaspoon kosher salt

2 cups all-purpose flour

2 cups raw walnut halves

3 cups confectioners' sugar

STORE: These cookies freeze well after being coated in sugar. Store them for up to 2 weeks in the freezer or in an airtight container at room temperature for 1 week.

This is one of Bono's favorite cookies. Yes, that Bono. The lead singer of U2, my absolute favorite band when I was growing up. These were on the cookie plate I served at Chateau Marmont in L.A., and he would always ask for the buttery, crumbly snowballs loaded with chunks of walnuts. He liked them so much they once inspired him to sing to me. I was nine months pregnant at the time, and to no one's surprise, I gave birth to my son the next day. I love to tell that story about Bono, but the delicate hint of cardamom is the real star of this cookie. As many of my customers have confessed, it's a perfect pairing with a glass of good port.

PREHEAT THE OVEN TO 325°F. LINE 2 BAKING TRAYS with nonstick baking mats or parchment paper.

In the bowl of a stand mixer fitted with a paddle attachment, beat the butter, granulated sugar, and cardamom until light and fluffy. The tenderness of the cookie depends on how much air you incorporate in this step. Add the vanilla and salt and beat until combined. Add the flour and beat on low speed until no streaks of flour remain. Scrape down the sides of the bowl with a rubber spatula as needed. Add the walnuts and continue to beat on low speed until evenly distributed and lightly crushed, about 30 seconds. Chill the dough for 45 minutes to 1 hour.

Spoon tablespoon-sized mounds of batter onto the prepared baking tray, spaced 1 inch apart. Bake for about 25 minutes, turning the pan halfway through baking, until golden brown. Allow the cookies to cool on the pan until they can be handled but are still warm to the touch, about 5 minutes.

Put the confectioners' sugar into a medium bowl. Gently lift each cookie from the baking tray and bury it in the sugar, until all the cookies are completely covered. Let the cookies cool completely in the sugar, about 10 minutes. That's the trick to getting the thick crust of powdered sugar that makes these cookies look like snowballs. Once cool, remove the cookies from the sugar and gently toss each cookie between your hands to shake off the excess sugar. (Sift the sugar left in the bowl and save it for future batches of cookies.)

When I worked at Craft restaurant in New York years ago with the talented pastry chef Karen DeMasco, I was responsible for preparing the poached rhubarb. It was a simple recipe of rhubarb, sugar syrup, and vanilla bean, but the combination was magical. Here, I've added fresh strawberries to tart rhubarb and aromatic vanilla bean to make a blushing pink tart with a fluffy brioche crust that would be an impressive addition to any brunch spread. The generous dose of ground ginger makes the brioche rich but not spicy—more kitchen magic.

Tart Dough

COMBINE THE MILK, YEAST, AND 1 TEASPOON SUGAR IN A small bowl. Let stand until foamy, about 5 minutes. Add the egg to the yeast mixture and whisk.

In the bowl of a stand mixer fitted with a paddle attachment, combine the flour, remaining 1 tablespoon sugar, the ground ginger, salt, and orange zest. Add the yeast mixture and beat on medium speed for 7 to 8 minutes, scraping once to help the flour incorporate into the mixture, until a dough forms. Pause occasionally to use a spatula to bring the dry crumbs from the bottom of the bowl to the top of the dough, and squeeze together the dough once or twice to help the dry crumbs incorporate. The dough won't be silky, and there may even be some dry crumbs at the bottom—that's okay. Slowly add the butter 1 teaspoon at a time, mixing on medium speed until each piece is incorporated before adding the next. This takes about 5 minutes. After 5 minutes the dough should form into a ball. It will begin to look very soft and elastic. Don't worry. It will come back together. The dough will form into a ball then separate as you continue to beat. This is okay. If it is still not coming together, you can add a bit of flour—a teaspoon at a time but no more than 3 teaspoons.

(Continued)

Blush Brioche Tart

ACTIVE TIME: 45 minutes
TOTAL TIME: 3 hours

Serves 8

TART DOUGH

2 tablespoons whole milk, warm to the touch but not hot, about 105°F

1¼ teaspoons active dry yeast

1 tablespoon plus 1 teaspoon granulated sugar

1 large egg plus 1 egg yolk, at room temperature (reserve white for egg wash)

1¼ cups all-purpose flour

½ teaspoon ground ginger

½ teaspoon kosher salt

¾ teaspoon finely grated orange zest

4 tablespoons (2 ounces) unsalted butter, at room temperature

MASCARPONE AND FRUIT FILLING

1 vanilla bean

1 cup mascarpone cheese, at room temperature

¾ pound rhubarb

8 ounces strawberries, hulled

¼ cup plus 2 tablespoons turbinado or granulated sugar

1 tablespoon tapioca flour or cornstarch

(Continued)

1 egg white (reserved from the dough)

Pinch of kosher salt

1 to 2 tablespoons unsalted butter, frozen and cut into small cubes

2 teaspoons turbinado or granulated sugar

Lightly flour your working surface. Turn the dough out onto the floured surface and knead the dough until it is smooth, 1 or 2 minutes. Transfer the dough to a medium-sized greased bowl and cover it with plastic wrap. Let the dough rise until it has doubled in size. This will take about 1 hour, depending on the room temperature. When the dough has doubled in size, punch it down and refrigerate the dough for 30 minutes to firm it. This step will prevent the butter from separating when baking.

Mascarpone and Fruit Filling

SLICE THE VANILLA BEAN LENGTHWISE AND SCRAPE OUT the seeds. Discard the pods or set aside for another use. In a bowl, combine the vanilla bean seeds with the mascarpone cheese. Cut rhubarb into ¼-inch slices. (If the rhubarb is very fat, cut it in half lengthwise before slicing.) Hull and halve the strawberries, leaving a few whole if the berries are small. Shortly before adding the filling to the tart, in a separate bowl, combine rhubarb, strawberries, sugar, and tapioca flour.

Assembling the Tart

PREHEAT THE OVEN TO 350°F. LINE A 13 × 18-INCH baking tray with a nonstick baking mat or parchment paper. Place the chilled dough on the nonstick baking mat or parchment and roll the dough across the pan into an oval about 13 inches by 6 inches. With your index and middle fingers, gently make a depression in the dough all around to create a 1-inch border. In a bowl, combine the egg white and salt to make an egg wash. Brush some of the egg wash onto the border of the oval, making a 1-inch-wide track. Spread the mascarpone filling evenly in the center of the oval and top with fruit filling. Dot the filling with frozen butter and sprinkle the border with sugar.

Bake for 30 minutes, rotate the baking tray, and bake until the crust is evenly browned, an additional 15 minutes. The edge will be golden brown. You can also lift the tart with a spatula to make sure the bottom is golden brown and cooked through. Allow to cool for 15 to 20 minutes. To serve, cut the tart lengthwise in half and then cut crosswise into 4 even pieces to make a total of 8 pieces.

Rose water is sweet and romantic. Espresso is bitter, even dirty. The combination is perfection. I like to use espresso powder in my cooking because it gives it an intense but smooth and balanced coffee flavor without the acidity of coffee. It's easy to keep both espresso powder and rose water on hand, and these two pantry items make these marshmallows the most sophisticated and heavenly you've ever had—a creamy latte inspired by the flavors of Turkey.

Raspberry-Rose Caramel

IN A COFFEE GRINDER, GRIND THE RASPBERRIES TO A fine powder. You should have about 1 tablespoon plus a teaspoon.

In a small saucepan over medium heat, combine the sugar, water, and corn syrup. Cook until light golden brown, 5 to 7 minutes. Add the cream and whisk to combine. Remove from the heat and stir in the raspberry powder, rose water, and salt. Strain the caramel through a fine-mesh sieve into a medium bowl. The caramel will look thin, but it will thicken as it cools.

Coffee Marshmallow Base

TO BLOOM THE GELATIN, PUT ½ CUP OF THE WATER INTO the bowl of a stand mixer fitted with a whisk attachment and sprinkle the gelatin over the water. Let the mixture rest until the gelatin has absorbed the water, about 10 minutes.

In a small saucepan, combine the granulated sugar, corn syrup, salt, and another ½ cup of the water. Cook the corn syrup mixture over medium heat until it registers 225°F on a candy thermometer. With the mixer on low speed, add the hot corn syrup mixture to the gelatin mixture, pouring it very slowly down the side of the bowl. When all the syrup has been added, increase the mixer speed to high and whip until the marshmallow mixture has tripled in volume, about 5 minutes. In a small bowl, stir together the espresso powder

(Continued)

Rose Latte Marshmallow Knots

ACTIVE TIME: 30 minutes
TOTAL TIME: Overnight

Makes 4 dozen marshmallows

RASPBERRY-ROSE CARAMEL

⅓ cup freeze-dried raspberries

⅓ cup granulated sugar

2 tablespoons water

1 teaspoon light corn syrup

3 tablespoons heavy cream

1½ teaspoons rose water

⅛ teaspoon kosher salt

COFFEE MARSHMALLOW BASE

1 tablespoon powdered gelatin

1 cup plus 1½ teaspoons cold water

¾ cup granulated sugar

½ cup light corn syrup

⅛ teaspoon kosher salt

2 tablespoons espresso powder

FINISHED MARSHMALLOWS

¾ cup confectioners' sugar

¼ cup cornstarch

SPECIAL EQUIPMENT

Deep fry/candy thermometer

Blowtorch (optional)

MAKE AHEAD: These are best
made 2 days in advance to
allow the marshmallows to dry
out slightly and form a crust.
If you can wait, this will make
them easier to knot.

STORE: The marshmallows can
be stored in a single layer in
an airtight container at room
temperature for up to 1 week.

and the remaining 1½ teaspoons water to make a paste. Add
the espresso paste to the mixer bowl and continue to beat
until the outside of the bowl cools to room temperature.

To put it all together

SIFT THE CONFECTIONERS' SUGAR AND CORNSTARCH
into a medium bowl. Whisk to combine. Sift ¼ cup of the
confectioners' sugar mixture evenly over an 8-inch square
pan. The pan should be completely covered. Reserve the
remaining sugar mixture.

Transfer half of the coffee marshmallow mixture into the
bowl of raspberry-rose caramel and fold gently to combine.
Transfer the caramel marshmallow mixture back into the
bowl of coffee marshmallow and fold gently 4 times to create
a ribbon of caramel marshmallow. Transfer to the prepared
pan and use an offset spatula to spread it out evenly. Let the
marshmallow rest, uncovered, at room temperature overnight.

Dust a cutting board with ¼ cup of the reserved sugar
mixture. Run a knife along the edge of the marshmallow and
turn the sheet of marshmallow out onto the cutting board.
Cut the marshmallow in half lengthwise, then turn the pan
and cut into 16 thin rows widthwise to make 4 dozen strips
measuring ½ inch by 4½ inches. Working in batches of 6,
toss the marshmallows in the remaining sugar mixture,
making sure each is completely covered. Tie each strip into a
knot, stretching the marshmallow as little as possible. Toss
the knots in any remaining sugar mixture. Place them in
single layers on a tray, stacked between parchment. Before
serving, shake each marshmallow in a strainer to remove any
extra sugar. These are also delicious charred with a blowtorch after tossing in sugar.

This is the perfect sweet roll: soft, fluffy dough; sticky, fruity cherry filling; gooey cream cheese frosting; and … something else. These basic sweet rolls are transformed into something alluring with just a few teaspoons of ground mahlab kernels, the pits of the sour St. Lucie cherry, which have a complex, fruity richness and a heavenly perfume. You'll be hooked even before the rolls come out of the oven. There aren't words to describe how much I love the smell of mahlab as it bakes. In Greece, Turkey, and the Middle East, mahlab is often used to flavor breads for festive occasions. You'll have everybody guessing about this hauntingly delicious flavor.

Swirled Cherry Sweet Rolls

ACTIVE TIME: 1 hour, 15 minutes
TOTAL TIME: 3 hours

Makes 9 rolls

Sweet Roll Dough

IN A CLEAN COFFEE GRINDER, GRIND THE MAHLAB KER-nels into a fine powder. Measure out 2¼ teaspoons freshly ground mahlab and set any extra aside for future use.

Into the bowl of a stand mixer fitted with a dough hook, add 1 tablespoon of the sugar, the yeast, and the milk and let sit until foamy, 5 to 7 minutes. Add the flour, butter, egg, salt, the remaining sugar, the lime zest, and the ground mahlab. Beat on low speed until dough forms. Increase the speed to medium and beat until silky and smooth, about 10 minutes. Transfer the dough into a large greased bowl, cover with plastic wrap, and allow to rise in a warm place until doubled in size, about 1½ hours.

Cherry Filling

IN A MEDIUM SAUCEPAN OVER MEDIUM-HIGH HEAT, combine the cherries, water, and sugar. Bring to a boil, then reduce the heat to medium and cook until cherries are soft, 12 to 15 minutes. Mash the cherries with a potato masher or a wooden spoon. Raise the heat to medium-high and cook until the mixture thickens to a jam-like consistency with no excess liquid at the bottom of the pan, 3 to 5 minutes, depending on how juicy the cherries are. Remove from the heat and add the lime juice, almond extract, and salt. Allow to cool. Makes a heaping ½ cup of cherry filling.

SWEET ROLL DOUGH

1 teaspoon whole mahlab kernels

⅓ cup granulated sugar, divided

2¼ teaspoons (1 package) active dry yeast

½ cup whole milk, warm to the touch but not hot, about 105°F

2 cups plus 2 tablespoons all-purpose flour

4 tablespoons (2 ounces) unsalted butter, at room temperature

1 large egg

¾ teaspoon kosher salt

2 teaspoons finely grated lime zest (reserve lime for juice; lemon can be substituted)

CHERRY FILLING

1 pound fresh sweet cherries, pitted (see Note)

2 tablespoons water

¼ cup granulated sugar

1 teaspoon freshly squeezed lime (or lemon) juice

¼ teaspoon almond extract

Pinch of kosher salt

(Continued)

(Continued)

FLORAL AND AROMATIC

Cream Cheese Frosting

USING AN ELECTRIC MIXER, BEAT TOGETHER THE CREAM cheese, sugar, and butter in a medium bowl until smooth. Add the salt, vanilla, and lime juice and beat to combine.

Assembling the Rolls

LINE AN 8-INCH SQUARE PAN WITH PARCHMENT PAPER and grease the paper. In a small bowl, make an egg wash by whisking the egg with the water and salt.

Punch down the dough and transfer onto a lightly floured piece of parchment paper cut to 11 by 15 inches or larger. Use a rolling pin to roll it into a rectangle 10 inches by 14 inches. If the dough rectangle is soft and difficult to handle, transfer parchment to a tray and refrigerate for 40 minutes.

Brush the top surface of the dough with half of the egg wash. Sprinkle the dough with the 2 tablespoons of sugar, leaving a 1-inch border uncovered. Spread the cherry filling over the dough, again being sure to leave a 1-inch border, then dot the dough with pieces of the butter. Starting from the long side, roll the dough tightly into a log. Pinch the dough along the long seam to seal. Cut the log into 9 equal rounds. (Tip: You can eyeball the 9 equally sized pieces or measure the log with a ruler and then divide.) Place the rounds, cut side up, evenly spaced, into the prepared pan. Cover with plastic wrap and let the dough rise until doubled in size, 30 minutes to 1 hour. Preheat the oven to 350°F.

After the dough has risen, brush the tops of the rolls with the remaining egg wash. Bake for 25 to 30 minutes, until golden. Allow to cool completely. Top with the cream cheese frosting.

NOTE: If buying ground mahlab, be sure to purchase it from a spice purveyor you know has a rapid turnover, as mahlab loses flavor quickly. You can also use frozen cherries for the filling. Thaw the cherries and press them in a sieve to extract as much juice as possible, about 1 cup. Reserve the juice for another use. Follow the instructions for cooking cherries, but you will need to cook them longer, about 8 to 10 minutes, to reach the consistency of jam.

STORE: These are best eaten the day they are made, but in a pinch you can make them 1 day ahead and store in the refrigerator. Allow them to come to room temperature before serving.

CREAM CHEESE FROSTING

3 ounces cream cheese, at room temperature

¾ cup confectioners' sugar, sifted

3 tablespoons (1½ ounces) unsalted butter, at room temperature

Pinch of kosher salt

¼ teaspoon vanilla extract

¼ teaspoon freshly squeezed lime (or lemon) juice

ASSEMBLING THE ROLLS

1 large egg

1 teaspoon water

Pinch of kosher salt

2 tablespoons granulated sugar

2 tablespoons (1 ounce) unsalted butter, at room temperature

Watermelon Jasmine Sherbet

ACTIVE TIME: 20 minutes
TOTAL TIME: 4 hours, 30 minutes

Makes 1 quart

1½ cups heavy cream, divided

1 tablespoon cornstarch

½ cup granulated sugar

¼ cup light corn syrup

¼ teaspoon kosher salt

2 teaspoons loose jasmine green tea

2½ pounds of watermelon,
including the rind

½ teaspoon freshly squeezed
lime juice

SPECIAL EQUIPMENT

Ice cream maker

Watermelon to me is *the* all-American summer fruit—juicy, messy, and delightful. It is there at every backyard barbecue, from the moment the weather gets warm until it's time to go back to school. It's best served ice cold, which, of course, makes me think of creating frozen desserts with it. Green tea flavored with alluring jasmine flowers makes this sherbet a little more grown-up than a big slice of watermelon, but it's just as refreshing.

IN A SMALL BOWL, WHISK TOGETHER 2 TABLESPOONS OF the heavy cream and the cornstarch and set aside. In a medium saucepan over medium-high heat, combine the remaining 1¼ cup plus 2 tablespoons heavy cream and the sugar, corn syrup, and salt and stir until the sugar is dissolved. When the cream mixture comes to a boil, remove it from the heat, stir in the jasmine tea, and cover. Allow the tea to steep for 5 minutes. (Steeping for longer will make the mixture bitter.) Strain the mixture through a fine-mesh sieve into another medium saucepan. Be sure to push all the liquid through the sieve, and discard the tea leaves. Whisk the cornstarch mixture into the cream mixture and set over medium-high heat. Bring to a boil and cook, whisking continuously, for 1 minute. Transfer the cream mixture to a medium bowl, cover, and refrigerate until cool, about 30 minutes.

Remove the rind from the watermelon and discard. Cut the flesh into ½-inch cubes. Working in batches, puree the watermelon in a blender until liquid. Strain through a fine-mesh sieve over a medium bowl to remove any solids. Measure out 2 cups of juice, and set aside any remaining to drink. Add the 2 cups juice to the chilled cream mixture and stir well to incorporate. Cover and refrigerate until very cold, about 2 hours or overnight. Stir in the lime juice.

Transfer the watermelon mixture to an ice cream maker and process according to the manufacturer's instructions. Freeze the sherbet until it is firm enough to scoop, about 2 hours.

STORE: Sherbet can be stored in an airtight container in the freezer for up to 2 weeks.

Sticky toffee pudding is my most famous—or most infamous—dessert. The recipe for that moist cake with sweet dates and deep, dark toffee sauce has traveled with me from New York to Los Angeles to Chicago, and it has devoted fans in every city. Now I want to share the secret with you: it's all about the sticky toffee sauce. These churros re-create the flavors of the original cake with date sugar and orange zest, and the semolina gives them an amazingly crispy texture. But the sticky toffee sauce with vanilla is the star. Use the best quality vanilla bean you can find. This is a recipe where it's worth the splurge for that wallop of fragrant vanilla. This sauce is so intoxicating you'll find yourself licking the bowl clean. When I owned a restaurant in Chicago, one couple admitted to me that the sticky toffee pudding was part of an evening ritual that ended with—well, you know. And, yes, it's that good.

Semolina Churros

SIFT TOGETHER THE SEMOLINA AND ALL-PURPOSE FLOUR into a small bowl.

In a medium saucepan, combine water, milk, butter, 1 tablespoon of the sugar, and the salt. Cook over medium-high heat until it comes to a boil. Remove the pan from the heat and immediately add the combined flours. Stir vigorously with a wooden spoon until the mixture is smooth and lump free. The dough will have the texture of a thick paste.

Transfer the dough to the bowl of a stand mixer fitted with a paddle attachment. Beat on low speed for 1 minute. The dough will release steam and cool slightly. Add the egg, vanilla, and orange zest and beat on medium speed until well incorporated, scraping down the sides of the bowl as needed. Cover the dough with a piece of plastic wrap pressed directly to its surface and refrigerate just until cooled to room temperature, about 15 minutes. In a small bowl, whisk together the remaining ½ cup of granulated sugar and the date sugar and cinnamon, then pour onto a shallow plate or pie tin and set aside. Make the toffee sauce while the dough is cooling.

(Continued)

Semolina Churros with Sticky Toffee Sauce

ACTIVE TIME: 40 minutes
TOTAL TIME: 1 hour

Serves 10

SEMOLINA CHURROS

⅓ cup fine semolina (not semolina flour, see In Your Pantry, page 11)

⅔ cup all-purpose flour

1 cup water

3 tablespoons whole milk

1 tablespoon unsalted butter

½ cup plus 1 tablespoon granulated sugar, divided

1 teaspoon kosher salt

1 large egg

½ teaspoon vanilla extract

¾ teaspoon finely grated orange zest

¼ cup date sugar

¼ teaspoon ground Vietnamese cinnamon

(Continued)

FLORAL AND AROMATIC

STICKY TOFFEE SAUCE

1 vanilla bean

6 tablespoons (3 ounces) unsalted butter

1 cup plus 2 tablespoons heavy cream

½ cup plus 2 tablespoons firmly packed dark muscovado sugar or dark brown sugar

⅛ teaspoon kosher salt

⅓ cup crème fraîche

2 quarts peanut oil

SPECIAL EQUIPMENT

Deep-fry/candy thermometer

¼-inch star tip

Sticky Toffee Sauce

SLICE THE VANILLA BEAN LENGTHWISE AND SCRAPE OUT the seeds. Discard the pods or set aside for another use. In a medium saucepan, combine the butter, cream, sugar, vanilla bean seeds, and salt. Bring to a boil over medium-high heat, whisking frequently, and then reduce heat to low and simmer for 3 minutes. Remove from the heat, whisk in the crème fraîche, and allow to cool.

To fry the churros and put it all together

ONCE THE CHURRO DOUGH HAS COOLED, POUR THE PEANUT oil into a large heavy-bottomed saucepan. The oil should be at least 2 inches deep. Using a candy thermometer to measure the temperature, heat the oil to 350°F.

Fill a large piping bag fitted with a ¼-inch star tip with churro dough. (You could also use a quart-size ziplock plastic bag and snip off one corner.) Pipe the churro dough directly into the hot oil, using kitchen scissors to snip off 4-inch lengths. Cut the dough at an angle. Work in batches, about 7 churros per batch. Fry each batch of churros, turning them often with tongs, until deep golden brown, 6 to 7 minutes. Remove the churros from the hot oil with your tongs. Drain for a few seconds on a stack of paper towels to absorb the excess oil, then roll the hot churros in the prepared plate of cinnamon sugar. Serve immediately with the toffee sauce on the side for dipping.

MAKE AHEAD: The mixed churro dough can be refrigerated for up to 2 days. Allow it to come to room temperature before continuing the recipe.

Lavender Brown Sugar Crunchies

My love for lavender desserts began with a taste of a remarkable lavender crème brûlée at Big Sur Bakery in California. Creamy chilled custard with a floral aroma and caramelized sugar on top—it was one of the simplest and most delicious creations I had ever had. After that, I started using lavender in my own baking. This cookie was a fixture on the cookie plate at my restaurant, Aigre Doux, in Chicago. The caramelized flavor of the brown sugar in these cookies is balanced by a generous amount of lemon. The cookies are great plain, but the fresh, herbaceous lavender glaze makes them really memorable.

ACTIVE TIME: 35 minutes
TOTAL TIME: 3 hours

Makes 3 dozen cookies

1 cup all-purpose flour

⅛ teaspoon kosher salt

8 tablespoons (4 ounces) unsalted butter, at room temperature

1½ teaspoons finely grated lemon zest

½ cup firmly packed dark brown sugar

1 tablespoon freshly squeezed lemon juice, divided

¼ cup whole milk

¼ teaspoon dried lavender buds, plus more for garnish, as needed

1 cup confectioners' sugar, sifted

SPECIAL EQUIPMENT
2-inch round cutter

IN A SMALL BOWL, WHISK TOGETHER THE FLOUR AND salt. In the bowl of a stand mixer fitted with a paddle attachment, beat the butter and lemon zest until fluffy. Add the brown sugar and beat well. Scrape down the sides of the mixer bowl. Add 1½ teaspoons of the lemon juice and beat at medium-low speed. Scrape down the sides of the bowl. Add the flour mixture all at once and beat on low speed until combined. Transfer the dough to a piece of parchment paper, cover the top with another piece of parchment, and use a rolling pin to roll the dough to ¼ inch thick. Chill for at least 2 hours and as long as overnight.

Position an oven rack in the lower third of the oven. Preheat the oven to 350°F. Line two baking trays with parchment paper or nonstick baking mats. Use a 2-inch round cookie cutter to cut out circles of dough. Transfer the dough circles onto the prepared baking trays. Gather up the excess scraps of dough, press into a ball, and reroll and cut. Put the baking trays into the refrigerator and chill until firm, about 10 minutes. Bake the chilled cookies for 8 to 10 minutes, rotating the pans halfway through baking, until golden and crisp. Transfer to a cooling rack.

(Continued)

MAKE AHEAD: The dough can be rolled out and cut into circles ahead of time. Wrap the dough circles tightly and store in the freezer for up to 1 month.

STORE: Baked, glazed cookies can be stored between sheets of parchment paper in an airtight container for up to 5 days.

While cookies are cooling, make the glaze. In a small saucepan over medium-high heat, combine the milk and lavender. Bring to a boil, then remove the pan from the heat, cover, and let steep for 15 minutes. Be careful not to infuse more; I suggest using a timer. Strain the infused milk through a fine-mesh sieve into a small bowl and discard the solids. Add the confectioners' sugar and whisk until smooth. Whisk in the remaining 1½ teaspoons lemon juice. Spread ½ teaspoon of glaze on each cookie, then sprinkle with additional lavender. Let the glaze set.

Crunchy Top Peach Cobbler

ACTIVE TIME: 20 minutes
TOTAL TIME: 1 hour, 20 minutes

Serves 6 to 8

1 pound peaches, pitted and cut into ½-inch slices, with skins on

¾ cup granulated sugar, divided

1 teaspoon freshly squeezed lemon juice

Seeds from ½ vanilla bean

1½ teaspoons tapioca flour

4 tablespoons (2 ounces) unsalted butter

¾ cup all-purpose flour

1½ teaspoons baking powder

½ teaspoon ground Vietnamese cinnamon

¼ teaspoon kosher salt

¾ cup buttermilk, at room temperature

1 teaspoon vanilla extract

1 cup fresh blueberries

2 tablespoons turbinado sugar

¼ teaspoon freshly grated nutmeg

Vanilla ice cream, to serve

Roasting or baking makes summer peaches even sweeter and caramelizes the natural sugars, deepening the fruit's flavor. Roasted peaches are one of the most sublime things you will ever taste. These magnificent peaches star in a simple cobbler made with nutty brown butter and crunchy nutmeg sugar. This is an easy dessert that comes together quickly but tastes like it took ages.

PREHEAT THE OVEN TO 350°F. LINE A BAKING TRAY WITH parchment paper to catch any drips and place a 9-inch pan on it.

In a large saucepan over medium heat, combine the peaches, 3 tablespoons of the granulated sugar, the lemon juice, and vanilla bean seeds. Bring to a simmer and cook for 1 minute. Remove from the heat and allow to cool. In a small bowl, whisk together 1 tablespoon of the granulated sugar and the tapioca flour.

In a small saucepan, melt the butter over medium-high heat and continue to cook until it begins to smell nutty, about 2 minutes. Swirl the pan and continue to cook until the butter is golden and dark brown flecks begin to appear, about 3 more minutes. Pour the browned butter into the 9-inch round pan.

In a medium bowl, whisk together the flour, the remaining ½ cup of granulated sugar, the baking powder, cinnamon, and salt. Add the buttermilk and vanilla extract and whisk just until batter forms. Using an ice cream scoop, deposit dollops of the batter in the round pan. You don't want to mix the dough with the brown butter, but it's okay if some butter seeps through. Add the tapioca-sugar mixture to the peaches in the saucepan and toss to coat. Scatter the peaches and juices over the dough. Scatter the blueberries on top of the peaches.

Bake for 25 minutes. While the cobbler is baking, mix together the turbinado sugar and nutmeg in a small bowl. Remove the pan from the oven and sprinkle the cobbler with the nutmeg sugar. Return the pan to the oven and bake for another 25 to 30 minutes, until golden brown. Serve warm or at room temperature with vanilla ice cream.

In my memories of Paris, the streets smell like French butter and sweet sugar. I can picture the patisserie windows packed with eye candy: fruits glistening with glaze, nestled in golden brown pastry. Frangipane, a classic French almond filling used in so many of those desserts, is one of my favorites. When I worked at Balthazar Bakery in New York, I made it numerous times every week. This recipe is studded with soft candied oranges and paired with robust figs. An aniseed sugar coats the crust and the fruit, setting off licorice fireworks with every bite.

Tartlet Dough

IN A BOWL, COMBINE THE FLOUR, SUGAR, AND SALT. With a pastry cutter or your hands, cut 3 tablespoons of butter into the dry mixture until it resembles a coarse meal. Add the remaining 6 tablespoons of the butter and cut into the mixture until the butter is pea-sized. Drizzle 3 tablespoons of water into the mixture and toss with your hands just until the dough holds together; you may not use all the water. If there are some dry patches in the dough, drizzle in additional water until dough forms. Shape the dough into a fat log 8 inches long. Wrap tightly in plastic wrap and rest for at least 1 hour.

Candied Orange Frangipane

IN A SMALL SAUCEPAN OVER MEDIUM HEAT, BROWN THE butter until nutty and dark brown. Allow it to cool. In the bowl of a standing mixer fitted with a paddle attachment, combine the almond flour, nutmeg, sugar, all-purpose flour, and salt. Add the egg, beating at low speed until blended. Add the brown butter and beat. Add the vanilla and candied orange zest and beat until combined. Refrigerate for at least 1 hour or overnight.

(Continued)

Fig and Candied Orange Tartlets

ACTIVE TIME: 50 minutes
TOTAL TIME: 3 hours

Serves 8

TARTLET DOUGH

1½ cups all-purpose flour

¾ teaspoon granulated sugar

¼ teaspoon kosher salt

9 tablespoons (4½ ounces) cold unsalted butter, cut into ½-inch cubes

3 to 5 tablespoons ice water

CANDIED ORANGE FRANGIPANE

6 tablespoons (3 ounces) unsalted butter

½ cup natural almond flour (blanched is a fine substitute)

Scant ⅛ teaspoon freshly grated nutmeg

3 tablespoons granulated sugar

1 tablespoon all-purpose flour

⅛ teaspoon kosher salt

1 large egg

½ teaspoon vanilla extract

(Continued)

5 tablespoons Candied Orange Zest
(page 26), cut into ¼-inch dice,
or substitute store-bought
candied orange (page 252) or
1 tablespoon finely grated orange zest

ASSEMBLING THE TARTLETS

1½ teaspoons aniseeds

1 tablespoon granulated sugar

½ teaspoon chopped
fresh thyme leaves

1 large egg

2 teaspoons water

Pinch of kosher salt

8 (about 12 ounces) black or green
ripe figs (or a combination),
cut in ½-inch slices

2 teaspoons butter,
at room temperature

Assembling the Tartlets

POSITION AN OVEN RACK IN THE MIDDLE OF THE OVEN.
Preheat the oven to 375°F.

In a skillet over medium heat, toast aniseeds until
fragrant, about 2 minutes. Using a mortar and pestle, lightly
crush the toasted aniseeds.

Remove the chilled dough from the refrigerator. Divide
the log in half, then divide each half into 4 equal pieces, for
8 pieces total. Form each piece of dough into a ball between
the palms of your hands. On a lightly floured surface, with a
rolling pin, gently roll the dough into 5-inch disks. Stack the
dough on a small tray with parchment between and refrigerate for at least 15 minutes, or until needed.

In a bowl, combine the sugar, aniseeds, and thyme,
rubbing the mixture between your fingers to release some of
the thyme's essential oils. In a separate bowl, prepare an egg
wash by whisking the egg with water and salt.

Remove the chilled disks from the refrigerator. Place
a heaping tablespoon of candied orange frangipane in the
center of each disk, leaving a 2-inch border. Brush the border
with egg wash. Place 4 or 5 fig slices in a tight circle, slightly
overlapping, on top of the frangipane. Brush the figs with
softened butter. Gently fold the tartlet dough edges up and
over the figs. Press the corners gently to seal. Chill for 15
minutes, then remove from the fridge and brush the pastry
with egg wash and sprinkle each tartlet generously with the
sugar mixture.

Bake the tartlets for 30 minutes. Turn the tray and bake
another 15 minutes, until the pastry is golden brown and the
figs have softened. Let cool before cutting. Serve warm or at
room temperature.

MAKE AHEAD: The dough can be made 1 day in advance and
refrigerated or frozen for up to 1 month and defrosted in the
refrigerator before use. The candied orange frangipane can be
refrigerated for up to 3 days.

STORE: The tartlets are best the day they are made, but they
can be stored tightly wrapped in plastic for up to 2 days in the
refrigerator. Reheat before serving.

If you are feeling impatient in early spring for a taste of summer, this is your recipe. Even if your berries are only okay, this will be great. Cooking half the strawberries intensifies its strawberry flavor, and the chamomile adds an extraordinary undertone of floral flavor. For me, though, this dessert isn't about summer. It's about weekend trips to my favorite childhood bakery. There was a strawberry tart there with three huge berries on the top, and the delicious fruit juices would drip into the custard and onto the crust. Even then, I knew it was a great combination, a more sophisticated take on strawberries and cream.

Angel Food Cubes

BEGIN BY MAKING THE ANGEL FOOD CAKE RECIPE. CUT the cake into 1-inch cubes until you have 4 cups of cake cubes. There will be a little cake left over. Enjoy it!

Strawberry-Chamomile Jam

IN A MEDIUM BOWL, STIR TOGETHER HALF OF THE strawberries (1 pound) with the sugar, chamomile, and lemon juice. Marinate for at least 1 hour and as long as overnight, to soften the berries and draw out their juices. Transfer the mixture to a medium saucepan and bring to a simmer, stirring every 2 or 3 minutes until reduced to 1 cup, about 12 to 15 minutes. Set aside to cool to room temperature. Slice the remaining strawberries horizontally into ¼-inch slices. Stir the strawberry slices into the cooled jam.

Creamy Custard

IN A SMALL SAUCEPAN OVER MEDIUM HEAT, COMBINE THE milk and ¼ cup of the brown sugar. Bring to a boil, then reduce the heat. In a medium bowl, whisk together the egg yolks, cornstarch, and the remaining ½ cup of sugar. Temper the egg mixture by adding a few tablespoons of the hot milk mixture to the bowl while whisking vigorously. This will warm but not cook the eggs. Add the remaining hot milk mixture slowly, whisking continuously. Return all the liquid

(Continued)

Strawberries and Cream Trifle

ACTIVE TIME: 1 hour, 30 minutes
TOTAL TIME: 2 hours

Serves 8 to 10

ANGEL FOOD CUBES

1 recipe Angel Food Cake (page 19), or store-bought angel food cake

STRAWBERRY-CHAMOMILE JAM

2 pounds strawberries, hulled

½ cup granulated sugar

2 tablespoons finely ground dried chamomile flowers, or approximately 4 chamomile tea bags

1 tablespoon freshly squeezed lemon juice

CREAMY CUSTARD

1 cup whole milk

¾ cup firmly packed light brown sugar, divided

Yolks from 4 large eggs

2 tablespoons cornstarch

1 ounce cream cheese, at room temperature

3 ounces mild, soft goat cheese, at room temperature

1½ teaspoons vanilla extract

1½ teaspoons freshly squeezed lemon juice

Pinch of kosher salt

(Continued)

VANILLA BEAN WHIPPED CREAM

1 vanilla bean, or
1 teaspoon vanilla extract

1 cup heavy cream

½ cup confectioners' sugar, sifted

LEMON SYRUP

3 tablespoons freshly squeezed
lemon juice

3 tablespoons granulated sugar

3 tablespoons water

to the saucepan. Cook over medium heat, whisking continuously, until thickened and bubbly, about 1 to 2 minutes. Remove the pan from the heat and strain over a medium bowl. Discard the solids. Add the cream cheese and goat cheese and whisk until smooth. Whisk in the vanilla, lemon juice, and salt. Cover the mixture with plastic wrap, pressing the plastic wrap against the surface. Chill in the refrigerator for 1 hour or overnight. Custard will thicken and set up.

Vanilla Bean Whipped Cream

SLICE THE VANILLA BEAN LENGTHWISE AND SCRAPE OUT the seeds. Discard the pods or set aside for another use. Put all the ingredients into the bowl of a stand mixer fitted with a whisk attachment. Whip until the cream is thick and forms soft peaks. Cover and chill until ready to use.

Lemon Syrup

COMBINE ALL THE INGREDIENTS IN A SMALL SAUCEPAN. Bring to a boil, then reduce the heat and simmer for 1 minute. Stir and set aside.

To put it all together

REMOVE THE CREAMY CUSTARD FROM THE REFRIGERATOR. Fold half of the whipped cream into the custard. Spread out the angel food cubes on a plate or tray and brush the cubes generously with lemon syrup.

Assemble the trifle in a 3-quart bowl. Start by spreading one-third of the strawberry-chamomile jam over the bottom of the bowl. Top with one-third of the creamy custard mixture, then one-third of the angel food cake cubes, and then one-third of the remaining whipped cream. Repeat two more times, layering the remaining strawberry-chamomile jam, creamy custard mixture, cake cubes, and whipped cream.

MAKE AHEAD: All the components of this dessert can be made ahead of time. The trifle itself can be made 1 day in advance and kept in the refrigerator. The trifle actually tastes better after it has "aged" for a day because the flavors have had time to marry. You can also make this in 8 to 10 individual servings in small glasses or dessert cups.

STORE: Store in the refrigerator. The trifle is best eaten within 2 days.

I can't resist chocolate and cardamom. The deep, dark flavor of chocolate gets a pick-me-up from floral cardamom. The flavors are delightful together in this light-as-air cookie I first created for *Food & Wine* magazine. This already perfect pairing gets even better with enigmatic hazelnuts and crunchy cocoa nibs, which have a deep chocolate flavor and temper the cookie's sweetness.

PREHEAT THE OVEN TO 350°F. TOAST THE HAZELNUTS ON a baking tray for about 14 minutes, until the skins blister. Be careful: they burn quickly. While the nuts are still warm, place them on a clean kitchen tea towel. Rub the nuts with the towel until most of the dark outer skins have been removed. Transfer the skinned nuts to a chopping board and roughly chop. Stir together the hazelnuts, cocoa powder, cornstarch, cocoa nibs, chocolate, and cardamom in a small bowl.

Reduce oven temperature to 300°F. Line a baking tray with parchment paper or a nonstick baking mat.

In the bowl of a stand mixer fitted with a whisk, whip the egg whites, cream of tartar, and salt. Whip on medium speed until soft peaks form, about 2 minutes. Continue to whip, adding the sugar in a slow stream. Whip until the whites are thick and glossy and hold their shape when the whip is removed, about 2 more minutes. Beat in the vanilla. Add the hazelnut mixture and fold in gently with a rubber spatula until combined. Don't overstir the meringue; you should still see streaks of cocoa.

Scoop 1 tablespoon of meringue onto the prepared baking tray. Place another 1-tablespoon scoop on top of the first. Repeat, creating equally spaced 2-scoop mounds with the remaining meringue. Bake for 15 minutes, turn the tray, and bake for 10 to 12 more minutes, until firm when tapped. Allow to cool on the pan. Once cooled, the meringues will have a crisp shell and a soft, creamy center.

STORE: These are best eaten the day they are made. They can be stored in an airtight container for up to 2 days.

Chocolate–Hazelnut Clouds

ACTIVE TIME: 15 minutes
TOTAL TIME: 35 minutes

 *Makes* 16 meringues

¼ cup whole hazelnuts with skin

1 tablespoon Dutch-process cocoa powder, sifted

2 teaspoons cornstarch

1½ teaspoons cocoa nibs

2 ounces bittersweet chocolate, finely chopped

Scant ¼ teaspoon ground cardamom, depending on your preference

Whites from 3 large eggs

⅛ teaspoon cream of tartar

Generous pinch of kosher salt

¾ cup granulated sugar

½ teaspoon vanilla extract

Elderflower Cordial

ACTIVE TIME: 30 minutes
TOTAL TIME: Overnight

Makes 6 cups

8 ounces fresh elderflowers,
white parts only
(don't use any brown flowers)

1 tablespoon finely grated lemon zest

1 tablespoon finely grated lime zest

6 cups boiling water

¾ cup freshly squeezed lemon juice

¼ cup freshly squeezed lime juice

3 cups granulated sugar

1 tablespoon citric acid (optional)

Growing up, I spent my summers in England visiting family. Memorable afternoons were spent playing on the backyard swing and sipping cold, fizzy elderflower and lemon drinks with my *bari ammi*, my grandmother, in her English rose garden. Now I make my own floral and tart cordial with sweetly scented elderflowers and citrus. (Why add citric acid? It's a natural preservative and gives a pleasant sour note.) You can mix it with ice-cold sparkling water for a refreshing summery drink or use it as a surprising sweetener for iced tea. It's also wonderful splashed onto a fruit salad or used as a soaking syrup for a simple pound cake.

COMBINE ELDERFLOWERS, LEMON ZEST, AND LIME ZEST in a medium bowl. Pour the boiling water over the elderflowers and allow to steep overnight.

Line a strainer with cheesecloth and place over a large saucepan. Strain the elderflower liquid into the pan and discard the solids. Add the lemon juice, lime juice, sugar, and citric acid, if using. Bring the liquid to a simmer and cook until the sugar is dissolved, 2 to 3 minutes. Pour the hot syrup into sterilized glass bottles or jars. Use the syrup whenever you want a taste of summer.

NOTE: To make homemade soda, combine 1 cup of sparkling water with ¼ cup plus 2 tablespoons of elderflower cordial and top with a few thin slices of lemon and lime.

STORE: Store in an airtight bottle in the refrigerator for up to 1 month.

I first experimented with this flavor combination for an event at the Culinary Institute of America in Napa. I knew I wanted to make a simple dessert, but I was hunting for an ingredient that would make it truly memorable. When I went into the kitchen, a box of Earl Grey was at the front of my cabinet. Of course it was: it's my favorite type of tea, and I start every morning with a hot cup. That combination of black tea and bergamot turned out to be just the thing my pavlova needed, too. The Earl Grey is subtle and delicious—and even better paired with a creamy chocolate filling.

Earl Grey Pavlova with Silky Chocolate Cream

ACTIVE TIME: 40 minutes
TOTAL TIME: 3 hours, 30 minutes

Serves 8 to 10

Silky Chocolate Cream

IN A MEDIUM SAUCEPAN OVER MEDIUM-HIGH HEAT, combine the milk and cream and bring to a simmer. In a medium bowl, beat the egg yolks. Slowly whisk the hot milk mixture into the beaten eggs, then transfer the mixture back into the saucepan. Cook the mixture over medium heat, whisking continuously, until slightly thickened, about 2 minutes. Turn off the heat and add the chocolate, stirring until the chocolate is completely melted. Stir in the salt and vanilla. Place a fine-mesh sieve over a medium bowl and strain the chocolate cream into the bowl. Refrigerate for at least 2 hours.

Earl Grey Meringue

PREHEAT THE OVEN TO 400°F. PLACE THE LOOSE TEA (or if using tea bags, cut the bags open and put tea) in a clean coffee grinder to grind the tea leaves into a fine powder.

In the bowl of a stand mixer fitted with a whisk attachment, whip the egg whites, cream of tartar, and vanilla on high speed until the mixture becomes foamy, about 2 minutes. Reduce speed to medium and gradually add the sugar in a steady stream. Increase the speed to high and beat until the whites are stiff and shiny, about 3 minutes. Sift the cornstarch over the whipped whites. Add the salt, orange zest, and ground tea and gently fold in with a rubber spatula to incorporate.

(Continued)

SILKY CHOCOLATE CREAM

¾ cup whole milk

¼ cup heavy cream

Yolks from 2 large eggs
(reserve the whites for the meringue)

6 ounces bittersweet chocolate,
roughly chopped

⅛ teaspoon kosher salt

½ teaspoon vanilla extract

EARL GREY MERINGUE

2 scant teaspoons best-quality
Earl Grey tea, or 2 tea bags

Whites from 3 large eggs,
at room temperature

⅛ teaspoon cream of tartar

½ teaspoon vanilla extract

¾ cup granulated sugar

(Continued)

2 teaspoons cornstarch

¼ teaspoon kosher salt

1½ teaspoons finely grated
orange zest

WHIPPED CREAM

1 cup heavy cream

½ cup confectioners' sugar, sifted

1 teaspoon vanilla extract

FOR THE GARNISH

½ to ¾ cup pomegranate seeds

1 large orange, supremed

Confectioners' sugar or
Dutch-process cocoa powder

Dab a little meringue in each corner of a baking tray. Cut a piece of parchment paper the size of the baking tray and trace a 7-inch circle in the center of the paper. Turn the paper upside down and place it on the baking tray, using the dabs of meringue to stick it in place as you work. Mound all the meringue into the center of the traced circle and use the back of a spoon to spread it to fill the circle. The meringue will be 2 to 3 inches thick and should have a slight depression in the middle. Don't worry about perfection.

Place the meringue in the oven and immediately reduce the temperature to 300°F. Bake for 30 minutes, turn the tray, and bake for an additional 15 minutes. Allow to cool completely in the pan. The meringue will be crisp on the outside and have a soft center.

Whipped Cream

COMBINE ALL THE INGREDIENTS IN THE BOWL OF A stand mixer fitted with a whisk attachment. Whip until the cream is thick and forms soft peaks. Chill until ready to assemble.

To put it all together

GENTLY LIFT THE EARL GREY MERINGUE WITH AN OFFSET spatula and transfer to a plate. To assemble the pavlova, mound the silky chocolate cream in the center of the Earl Grey pavlova and spread it out evenly, leaving a 1½- to 2-inch border. (If the middle of the meringue puffed during baking, push it down to make room for the chocolate cream.) Top with the whipped cream and garnish with pomegranate seeds and orange segments. Dust with confectioners' sugar and serve immediately.

MAKE AHEAD: You can make all the separate components up to 1 day in advance. Meringue should be wrapped airtight and other items should be refrigerated until ready to assemble.

Candied violets seem exotic in the United States, but they've been a standard in European sweets for centuries. They have a delicate floral aroma and an inimitable sweetness. Once you taste them, you'll want to keep your pantry stocked. In this ice cream, the crunchy, candied flowers complement the creamy freshness and tang of the lemon. This ice cream is beautifully balanced—tangy and floral.

Lemony Lemon Ripple Ice Cream

ACTIVE TIME: 15 minutes
TOTAL TIME: Overnight

Makes 1 quart

Buttermilk Ice Cream Base

IN A MEDIUM SAUCEPAN, COMBINE THE HEAVY CREAM and ½ cup of the sugar. Bring the mixture to a simmer over medium-high heat. While the cream is heating, whisk together the egg yolks and remaining ¼ cup sugar in a medium bowl. When the cream mixture comes to a simmer, pour about half the cream mixture slowly into the egg mixture, whisking continuously to combine. Pour the warm egg mixture back into the saucepan with the remaining milk mixture. Cook over low heat, stirring continuously with a spatula, until the custard thickens enough to coat the back of the spatula, about 5 minutes. Strain the custard through a fine-mesh sieve into a medium bowl. Cover and refrigerate until it comes to room temperature. Add the buttermilk and salt and stir to combine. (Cooling the mixture before adding the buttermilk is important. Otherwise, the buttermilk will curdle.) Chill in a covered container in the refrigerator until very cold, several hours or overnight.

Transfer the custard to an ice cream maker and process according to the manufacturer's instructions.

(Continued)

BUTTERMILK ICE CREAM BASE

1½ cups heavy cream

¾ cup granulated sugar, divided

Yolks from 6 large eggs

1½ cups buttermilk

⅛ teaspoon kosher salt

LEMON CURD

½ cup granulated sugar

1½ teaspoons finely grated lemon zest

⅓ cup freshly squeezed lemon juice

Yolks from 4 large eggs

5 tablespoons (2½ ounces) unsalted butter, at room temperature and cut into cubes

2 tablespoons plus 2 teaspoons candied violet pieces, roughly chopped

SPECIAL EQUIPMENT

Ice cream maker

Lemon Curd

IN A DOUBLE BOILER, WHISK TOGETHER THE SUGAR, lemon zest, lemon juice, and egg yolks. Cook over low heat, stirring frequently, until the lemon custard is thick enough to coat the back of a spoon well, about 25 minutes. Strain the custard through a fine-mesh sieve into a medium bowl and let it stand for 7 to 8 minutes to cool before adding the butter. Add the butter in small amounts, whisking between additions to emulsify the curd. (You can use an immersion blender for this step to achieve a very creamy curd.) Cover the bowl with plastic wrap pressed directly on the surface of the lemon curd to prevent a skin from forming. Chill in the refrigerator until very cold, at least 2 hours.

To put it all together

CHILL A LARGE METAL BOWL IN THE FREEZER UNTIL ICY to the touch, about 15 minutes. Scoop about one-third of the freshly churned buttermilk ice cream into the bowl and spread it out in an even layer. Spoon about one-third of the lemon curd on top of the ice cream and sprinkle with about one-third of the candied violet. Repeat twice more with remaining ice cream, lemon curd, and candied violet. With a spatula, gently fold the ice cream 4 times to create ribbons of lemon curd through the ice cream. Don't be overzealous with the mixing. Cover the bowl with plastic wrap pressed to the surface of the ice cream and freeze until firm enough to scoop, at least 3 hours.

STORE: Ice cream can be stored in an airtight container in the freezer for up to 2 weeks.

Floral-Kissed Kumquat Preserves

ACTIVE TIME: 2 hours, 20 minutes
TOTAL TIME: 2 days

 Makes 3 cups

---

2 lemons

1 pound kumquats

5½ cups water

4 medium-sized fresh bay leaves

3 cups granulated sugar

½ teaspoon kosher salt

1 teaspoon orange blossom water

SPECIAL EQUIPMENT

Deep-fry/candy thermometer
(optional)

I have wonderful childhood memories of freshly baked multigrain bread, toasted until crisp and slathered with butter and bittersweet marmalade. Marmalade was a favorite of my abbu and amma, and my aunt Fawzi khala would make jars of it for us every year. This version uses orange blossom water, made from bitter oranges and orange blossoms. It's a fruity and floral kiss with a pleasantly bitter aftertaste. But it's potent—a little goes a long way. There are bay leaves here, too. The bay gives this marmalade an intriguing depth of flavor, but it isn't the star.

WASH THE LEMONS AND KUMQUATS. CUT THE LEMONS IN half lengthwise and trim off the ends. Slice into extremely thin half-moon slices, about 1/16 inch thick. Remove the seeds and reserve. Slice the kumquats into thin rounds, about ⅛ inch thick. Remove the seeds and reserve. Place the sliced lemons and kumquats in a saucepan with a capacity of at least 3 quarts. Cover the citrus with cold water and bring to a boil over high heat. Remove from the heat and drain. Return the lemon and kumquat slices to the pan and add the 5½ cups of water and the bay leaves. Use a piece of cheese-cloth to make a sachet with the reserved citrus seeds inside and add it to the pan. Bring the mixture to a boil, then cover and remove from the heat. Refrigerate the mixture overnight to allow the natural pectin in the fruit and seeds to thicken it. The next day, the liquid will be slightly viscous.

Return the pan to the stove and add the sugar and salt. Bring to a simmer over medium heat and then cook for 40 minutes, stirring occasionally. Remove from the heat. Remove the seed sachet and place on a plate to cool. When the sachet is cool enough to handle, squeeze it over the pan to return any liquid to the pan.

(Continued)

NOTE: You can also test the marmalade without a thermometer: Chill a small plate in the freezer until very cold, about 5 minutes. Spoon a little bit of marmalade onto the chilled plate and wait 2 to 3 minutes. Nudge the puddle of marmalade with the edge of a spoon. If it wrinkles a bit and appears thickened, it's done.

STORE: The marmalade can be stored in airtight jars in the refrigerator for up to 1 month. Alternatively, try canning it, following your canner's directions for marmalade.

Return the pan to the stove again and cook over medium heat, stirring more frequently to avoid scorching, until the marmalade reaches 215°F to 220°F on a candy thermometer, about 1 hour. Remove the pan from the heat and pour the marmalade into a large bowl to cool. Cover with plastic wrap pressed directly onto the surface of the marmalade to prevent a skin from forming. Once the preserves have cooled completely, remove the bay leaves and stir in the orange blossom water.

These rose-scented scones turn breakfast into an episode of *Downton Abbey*. They always make me feel like I should be drinking tea with my pinky in the air. There's just something about cooking with rose water and dried rose petals that makes everything more refined and elegant and a little bit romantic. The secret is subtlety. If you've ever had a dessert that tasted like potpourri, you know how important that is. In these scones, the rose is quiet and proper, but those little bursts of fresh pomegranate shout.

PREHEAT THE OVEN TO 350°F. LINE A BAKING TRAY WITH a nonstick baking mat or parchment paper.

In a large bowl, whisk together the flour, ¼ cup plus 2 tablespoons of the sugar, the baking powder, and the salt. Add the butter, tossing to coat the cubes in the flour mixture. Place the bowl in the freezer and chill until the butter is very cold, about 15 minutes. Use your fingers or a pastry cutter to break the cold butter into small, pea-sized bits. Stir in the milk chocolate. In a medium bowl, whisk together the egg, 1 cup of the cream, and the rose water. Add the cream mixture to the flour mixture and toss with your hands to form a rough dough.

Lightly flour your work surface and turn the dough out onto it. With a rolling pin, roll the dough into a 12-inch circle. Scatter pomegranate seeds over half of the dough and fold the other half of the dough over the pomegranate seeds. Gently knead the dough 4 or 5 times, folding the dough onto itself, to incorporate the pomegranate seeds. Roll the dough into an 8-inch circle about 1 inch thick. Cut out circular scones with a 2-inch biscuit cutter. Then very gently gather the dough scraps together and reroll and cut. Transfer scones to the prepared baking tray and refrigerate until firm, about 30 minutes.

(Continued)

Pomegranate Milk Chocolate Scones

ACTIVE TIME: 25 minutes
TOTAL TIME: 1 hour, 30 minutes

Makes 15 scones

3 cups all-purpose flour
(chilled for at least 15 minutes)

½ cup granulated sugar, divided

1 tablespoon baking powder

½ teaspoon kosher salt

8 tablespoons (4 ounces)
cold unsalted butter,
cut into ½-inch cubes

4 ounces milk chocolate,
roughly chopped

1 large egg, cold

1 cup plus 2 tablespoons
chilled heavy cream

2¼ teaspoons rose water

1 cup fresh pomegranate seeds

2 teaspoons dried rose petals, crushed

SPECIAL EQUIPMENT

2-inch round cutter

Brush the chilled scones lightly with the remaining 2 tablespoons of cream. In a small bowl, stir together the remaining 2 tablespoons of sugar and the rose petals. Sprinkle about ½ teaspoon of the rose sugar on top of each scone. Bake for 18 to 20 minutes, until a wooden toothpick inserted into the center of a scone comes out clean.

NOTE: The trick to great scones is using very cold ingredients and handling the dough as little as possible.

MAKE AHEAD: The dough can be made 1 day in advance and stored in the refrigerator. The scones can also be cut out 1 day ahead, and frozen. Wait until just before baking to add the rose sugar.

Roasted Peach and Custard Borek

ACTIVE TIME: 35 minutes
TOTAL TIME: 1 hour, 30 minutes

Makes 8 pieces

CREAMY SAFFRON CUSTARD

2 tablespoons heavy cream

1 cup plus 2 tablespoons whole milk

¼ cup granulated sugar, divided

Scant ¼ teaspoon saffron threads

One 1-inch strip lemon peel

⅛ teaspoon kosher salt

2 tablespoons cornstarch

Yolks from 2 large eggs

1 tablespoon unsalted butter

½ teaspoon vanilla extract

TURNOVERS

¼ cup granulated sugar

¼ teaspoon ground cardamom

¼ teaspoon kosher salt

½ large peach

Four 13 × 16-inch phyllo sheets, defrosted in the refrigerator

About 4 tablespoons (2 ounces) unsalted butter, melted

HONEY BUTTER GLAZE

1 tablespoon unsalted butter, melted

2 tablespoons mild honey

This dessert was inspired by one made famous by the pastry chef Gina DePalma at Babbo in New York: saffron panna cotta with roasted peaches. I worked for Gina early in my career, when she was heading the kitchen at Cub Room. Her panna cotta was delicate and creamy, and the saffron made it unforgettable. Here, I combine peaches with a velvety saffron cream and subtle cardamom sugar, all wrapped inside light, crunchy layers of phyllo dough. Finally, the turnovers are brushed with honey butter, which creates a beautiful lacquered finish with an addictive toffee-like taste. You'll be picking at every last crunchy bit left on the tray.

Creamy Saffron Custard

IN A MEDIUM SAUCEPAN OVER MEDIUM HIGH HEAT, combine the cream, milk, 2 tablespoons of the sugar, the saffron, and the lemon peel. Bring to a boil and then remove from the heat, cover, and allow to infuse for 30 minutes. Remove the lemon peel and bring the mixture back to a boil.

In a medium bowl, whisk together the remaining 2 tablespoons sugar and the salt, cornstarch, and egg yolks until smooth. Place a fine-mesh sieve over a separate medium bowl and set aside for later use. Temper the egg mixture by adding a few tablespoons of the hot cream mixture to the bowl while whisking vigorously. This will warm but not cook the eggs. Add the remaining hot cream mixture slowly, whisking continuously. Pour the mixture back into the saucepan and bring to a boil over medium-high heat, whisking continuously. Reduce the heat to medium and cook, whisking continuously, until the mixture is very thick, about 4 minutes. With a rubber spatula, scrape the mixture into the prepared sieve and use the spatula to press the custard through the sieve to remove any lumps. Add the butter and vanilla to the strained custard and whisk until well combined. Cover with a piece of plastic wrap pressed directly to the surface of the custard and pierce the plastic wrap with a knife to allow steam to escape. Refrigerate until well chilled, at least several hours.

(Continued)

Turnovers

PREHEAT THE OVEN TO 375°F. LINE A BAKING TRAY WITH a nonstick baking mat. In a small bowl, whisk together the sugar, cardamom, and salt. Cut the peach half into ⅛-inch-thick slices and then cut those slices in half.

Unroll the phyllo dough. Cover the sheets of dough with a piece of plastic wrap followed by a barely damp kitchen towel to prevent the dough from drying out. (Don't let the damp towel touch the dough.) Working quickly, lift the plastic wrap and towel to remove 1 sheet of phyllo dough and lay it on the countertop. Carefully re-cover the remaining dough. Brush the sheet lightly with melted butter. Sprinkle 1 tablespoon of the cardamom-sugar mixture evenly over it. Top with another sheet of phyllo dough and pound on the top sheet with the palm of your hand to adhere the sheets to each other. Brush the top with butter and sprinkle with another 1 tablespoon of the cardamom-sugar mixture. Repeat until four sheets of the phyllo dough have been stacked and topped. Cut lengthwise into 4 equal strips. Close to the bottom of each strip, place 1½ teaspoons of the saffron custard. Top with a piece of peach, then another 1½ teaspoons of the saffron custard and another piece of peach.

Starting with the bottom left-hand corner of one strip, fold the dough over the filling to meet the opposite edge, forming a triangle. Then fold this triangular pocket of dough directly away from you, then toward the left, then directly away from you, wrapping the triangle in dough. Continue until you reach the end of the strip. Brush the end of the dough lightly with butter and fold over to seal the turnover. Place the turnover on the prepared baking tray with the sealed edge on the bottom. Brush the top lightly with butter. Repeat the process for the remaining 3 strips. Space turnovers at least ½ inch apart.

Start the process over with a new sheet of phyllo dough, brushing all 4 remaining sheets of dough with butter and sprinkling with cardamom-sugar mixture. Cut into strips, fill, and fold as above. Bake for 10 minutes.

Honey Butter Glaze

WHILE THE TURNOVERS ARE BAKING, MEASURE THE remaining melted butter used for brushing. Add additional butter as needed to equal 1 tablespoon. In a small saucepan over medium heat, heat butter and honey until they come to a boil; immediately turn heat off. After the turnovers have baked for 10 minutes, remove from the oven and brush with the hot honey glaze. Rotate the pan and return to the oven. Continue to bake the turnovers for about 15 minutes, until their surfaces are shiny, caramelized, and deeply golden. Let cool for at least 15 minutes before serving. The turnovers will stay crunchy for several hours, but they are best served the day they are baked.

MAKE AHEAD: The saffron custard can be made up to 2 days in advance.

FLORAL AND AROMATIC

Creamy Horchata Ice Cream

I developed a love for horchata when I lived in L.A., one of the best places in the country for Mexican food. My oldest son loves it, too, and a tall, iced horchata was a must after a hot afternoon at the park. It might be even better as an ice cream, made with intensely floral Ceylon cinnamon and distinctively nutty and aromatic basmati rice. Using the Ceylon cinnamon, also known as Mexican cinnamon, is traditional, but adding the "King of Rice" instead of plain long-grain white rice is definitely untraditional. The combination of aromas is divine, and the natural starch in the rice makes the ice cream especially creamy.

ACTIVE TIME: 20 minutes
TOTAL TIME: Overnight

Makes 3 cups

½ cup whole almonds with skin, roughly chopped

½ cup basmati rice

One 4-inch Ceylon cinnamon stick

2½ cups whole milk

1½ cups heavy cream

½ vanilla bean

Yolks from 5 large eggs

¾ cup granulated sugar

¾ teaspoon kosher salt

SPECIAL EQUIPMENT

Ice cream maker

IN A LARGE 10- OR 12-INCH CAST IRON SKILLET OVER high heat, toast the almonds, rice, and cinnamon stick, stirring frequently, until the almonds are fragrant, about 3 minutes. Transfer the toasted mixture to a large saucepan and add the milk and heavy cream. Cut the vanilla bean lengthwise, if not cut lengthwise already, and scrape out the seeds. Add the seeds and pod to the saucepan. Over low heat, bring the milk mixture to a simmer. Remove the pan from the heat, cover, and let steep for 2 hours.

Strain the mixture through a fine-mesh sieve into a medium saucepan. Be sure to squeeze as much liquid as possible from the rice. You should have about 2½ cups of the milk mixture. Discard the solids. Bring the milk mixture to a boil over high heat. While it is heating, whisk together the egg yolks and sugar in a medium bowl. When the milk mixture comes to a boil, pour half the hot liquid slowly into the egg mixture, whisking continuously to combine. Pour the warm egg mixture back into the saucepan with the remaining milk mixture. Cook over low heat, stirring continuously with a spatula, until the custard thickens enough to coat the back of the spatula, about 5 minutes. Add the salt and strain the custard through a fine-mesh sieve. Chill in a covered container in the refrigerator until very cold, several hours or overnight.

Transfer the custard to an ice cream maker and process according to the manufacturer's instructions. Freeze the ice cream for 3 to 4 hours, until it is firm enough to scoop.

STORE: Ice cream can be stored in an airtight container in the freezer for up to 2 weeks.

REMEMBER THE EXACT MOMENT THAT I FIRST TRIED HERBS IN A dessert. It was at Gramercy Tavern in New York when my mentor Claudia Fleming was at the helm of the pastry kitchen. She served a creamy, rich coconut milk pudding with a tart passion fruit sorbet and passion fruit caramel finished with a drizzle of grass-green cilantro syrup. Cilantro in my dessert? Yes, please. I was a young pastry chef, and I fell in love with the vivid, fresh flavors herbs could bring to baking. Suddenly, I realized: you can use herbs like lemongrass the same way you use spices, and you can reimagine traditionally savory spices like puckery sumac for sweets.

The possibilities are limitless.

Bright *and* Fresh

Lemon Verbena Chiffon Roll

ACTIVE TIME: 30 minutes
TOTAL TIME: Overnight

Serves 10 to 12

ALMOND CAKE

½ cup sliced almonds with skin,
or blanched

1½ cups granulated sugar, divided

1 cup all-purpose flour

1 teaspoon baking powder

1 teaspoon baking soda

¼ teaspoon kosher salt

4 large eggs plus 2 egg whites,
at room temperature

½ cup grapeseed oil

½ cup water, at room temperature

2 teaspoons vanilla extract

½ teaspoon finely grated lemon zest

LEMON SYRUP

⅓ cup freshly squeezed lemon juice

⅓ cup granulated sugar

LEMON VERBENA WHIPPED CREAM

1¼ cups heavy cream

¼ cup firmly packed,
torn fresh lemon verbena leaves
(see Resources, page 252)

½ cup confectioners' sugar

(Continued)

Whipped cream is, quite simply, one of the best foods there is. The only thing better than whipped cream? Lemon verbena whipped cream. The cream is the perfect foil for the distinctive perfume and sunny, floral notes of this herb, which is herbal and lemony but not acidic. I've rolled up this fluffy, fragrant whipped cream in moist almond cake. The unexpected combination is superb.

Almond Cake

PREHEAT THE OVEN TO 325°F. TOAST THE SLICED almonds on a baking tray for 7 to 8 minutes, until lightly browned. Let the almonds cool on the tray, then transfer them to a large cutting board and roughly chop them into small pieces with a knife.

Increase the oven temperature to 350°F. Grease the bottom and sides of a 13 × 18-inch baking tray with grapeseed oil. Line the tray with parchment paper and grease the parchment paper.

In a medium bowl, sift together 1 cup of the sugar and the flour, baking powder, baking soda, and salt. Whisk in the crushed almonds. Separate all the egg yolks from the egg whites. In a large bowl, whisk together 4 of the egg yolks and the grapeseed oil, water, vanilla, and lemon zest until smooth. Slowly add the flour mixture to the egg yolk mixture, whisking gently until incorporated.

In the bowl of a stand mixer fitted with a whisk attachment, whip the 6 egg whites on low speed until slightly foamy. Increase the speed to medium and slowly add the remaining ½ cup of sugar in a slow stream, beating until the whites are thick and shiny and hold peaks. Fold one-third of the whites mixture into the yolk batter to lighten it, then gently fold in the remaining whites.

Pour the batter into the prepared baking tray, scraping any remaining batter from the bowl. Use an offset spatula to spread the batter evenly in the pan. Bake until the edges of the cake start to pull away from the sides of the pan. Allow to cool to room temperature in the baking tray.

(Continued)

2 tablespoons confectioners' sugar

1 cup raspberries, strawberries, or mixed berries (optional)

Lemon Syrup

IN A SMALL SAUCEPAN OVER MEDIUM-HIGH HEAT, combine the lemon juice and sugar. Bring to a boil, reduce the heat to medium low, and simmer until slightly syrupy, 2 to 3 minutes. Set aside.

Lemon Verbena Whipped Cream

IN A SMALL SAUCEPAN OVER MEDIUM-HIGH HEAT, combine the cream and lemon verbena. Bring to a boil, then turn off the heat, cover, and let steep for 30 minutes. Strain the mixture through a fine-mesh sieve into a small bowl and discard the solids. Chill for at least 4 hours and as long as overnight. (If the cream is not very cold, it won't whip well.) Transfer to the bowl of a stand mixer fitted with a whisk attachment and add the confectioners' sugar. Whip until medium peaks form.

Assembling the Roll

TO REMOVE THE CAKE FROM THE BAKING TRAY, LIGHTLY sift 1 tablespoon of the confectioners' sugar over the cake. Cover the cake with a piece of parchment paper and then place another baking tray on top of the paper, bottom down. Holding both trays, invert the cake onto the upside-down baking tray. Remove the original baking tray and peel the parchment paper off the bottom of the cake. Replace the parchment loosely over the cake. Invert the cake again onto the bottom of the original tray so it is right-side up, remove the second tray and parchment paper from the top, then slide the cake off the tray onto the countertop.

Trim the edges of the cake slightly, removing about ¼ inch. Brush the cake with the lemon syrup. With an offset spatula, spread the lemon verbena whipped cream evenly over the cake, leaving a 1-inch border on all sides. If using berries, scatter them over the cream. Arrange the cake so the long sides are parallel with the edge of the countertop. Using the parchment paper to help, gently roll the cake to create a long, even roll. Use the parchment paper to transfer the rolled cake onto a platter, seam down. Wrap well with plastic wrap and chill for at least 2 hours and as long as overnight. Sift the remaining 1 tablespoon of confectioners' sugar over the cake before serving.

Hibiscus Tamarind Spritzer

At a dinner party, a friend served me a beautiful, deep magenta colored beverage. After one sip of the mysterious liquid, I had to ask what was in it. It was tart and slightly sour, with just the right balance of sweetness to make it refreshing and memorable. The answer: hibiscus and tamarind. This is my take on that combination, with an added hint of clove. It's a thirst quencher with still or sparkling water. Or you can use the syrup in cocktails, toss it with some fresh berries, or drizzle it over your morning French toast.

ACTIVE TIME: 30 minutes
TOTAL TIME: Overnight

Makes 2½ quarts

4 ounces whole fresh tamarind pods

1 cup plus 2 quarts water, divided

3½ ounces dried hibiscus flowers

Five 4½-inch strips orange peel, white pith removed

6 whole cloves

3 to 3½ cups firmly packed light brown sugar

2 to 3 cups cold sparkling or still water

Fresh mint leaves, for garnish

TO PREPARE THE TAMARIND, REMOVE THE OUTER HARD shell of the pods with your fingers as well as the sturdy fibers that enclose the fruit. Break each tamarind into 3 or 4 pieces. Place the tamarind fruit and 1 cup of the water in a small saucepan and bring to a boil over medium-high heat. Reduce the heat to low, cover, and simmer until the tamarind softens, about 10 minutes. The seeds should loosen from the pulp; you can use a wooden spoon to help things along. The mixture will resemble a puree at this point. Cover and refrigerate overnight.

Meanwhile, in a large saucepan, combine the remaining 2 quarts of water and the hibiscus, orange peel, cloves, and brown sugar. Bring to a boil over medium-high heat. Reduce the heat to medium and simmer for 1 minute. Remove the pan from the heat, cover, and let the mixture stand overnight at room temperature to steep.

The next day, whisk the cooked tamarind into the steeped hibiscus and bring to a simmer over medium-high heat. Immediately take the mixture off the heat and strain through a fine-mesh sieve over a large bowl. Discard the solids. Chill the syrup in the refrigerator. When ready to serve, add sparkling or still water to taste, then add ice. Garnish with mint leaves.

STORE: The syrup can be stored in an airtight container in the refrigerator for up to 2 weeks.

Mulled Cider

ACTIVE TIME: 10 minutes
TOTAL TIME: 1 hour, 10 minutes

 6 cups

½ gallon fresh apple cider

¼ teaspoon black peppercorns

1 tablespoon plus 1 teaspoon
allspice berries

16 whole cloves

Four 3-inch cinnamon sticks

¼ teaspoon freshly grated nutmeg

3 star anise pods

1 teaspoon coriander seeds

Four 1 × 4-inch strips orange peel,
white pith removed

Spiced cider is traditional fall fare, warm and comforting with allspice, cloves, nutmeg, and cinnamon. But I like to add a few extra spices: star anise for its hint of licorice, coriander seeds for a citrus twang and muskiness, and black pepper for its little spark of heat. The finished cider is both familiar and exciting.

IN A LARGE SAUCEPAN, COMBINE ALL THE INGREDIENTS. Bring the cider to a boil over high heat, then reduce the heat to medium-low and simmer gently for 30 minutes. Cover the saucepan and allow the cider to steep for 1 hour. (Allowing the spices to steep for longer can make the mixture bitter.) Strain the cider and discard the spices. Serve hot.

NOTE: If you have leftover apple cider, turn it into candy. There's a recipe for Apple Cider Jellies on page 216.

STORE: The strained cider can be stored in the refrigerator for up to 1 week.

These truffles are both dark and bright. The first bite hits you with the citrus tang of passion fruit, which is followed by the intense aromas of the kaffir lime leaves. The brightness lingers, even as it melds with the slightly fruity and deep, dark, bitter notes of a good-quality chocolate. (Choose one you really like for this recipe.) It's a seductive combination.

LINE A 9 × 5-INCH LOAF PAN WITH A PIECE OF ALUMINUM foil large enough to create a 2-inch overhang on all sides. Grease lightly with a neutral oil or cooking spray.

In a small saucepan over medium-high heat, combine the cream and lime leaves. Bring to a boil, then immediately remove from the heat, cover, and let steep for 30 minutes. (Set a timer so you don't forget or oversteep.) Strain the infused cream through a fine-mesh sieve into a small bowl and set aside. Discard the lime leaves.

Cut the passion fruits in half and use a spoon to scrape out all the orange flesh and seeds into the bowl of a food processor. Pulse until the pulp has loosened from the seeds. Pour the passion fruit into a fine-mesh sieve set over a medium bowl and use a spatula to press the pulp through, being sure to get all the juice. Discard the seeds. Measure out 3 tablespoons plus 2 teaspoons of juice.

In a double boiler, combine the passion fruit juice, chocolate, butter, sugar, vanilla, and salt. Add the infused cream. Cook over medium heat, stirring occasionally, until the chocolate is completely melted. The mixture will appear broken. Transfer the mixture to a food processor and process until it forms a thick and glossy ganache, about 2 minutes. (You can also use an immersion blender to emulsify the ganache.) Pour the ganache into the prepared pan and gently tap the bottom of the pan against the countertop to remove air bubbles. Cover with plastic wrap and refrigerate until the truffles are firm, at least 2 hours and as long as overnight.

(Continued)

Fudgy Passion Fruit Truffles

ACTIVE TIME: 20 minutes
TOTAL TIME: 3 hours

Makes 32 truffles

²⁄₃ cup heavy cream

1½ teaspoons finely chopped fresh kaffir lime leaves (3 to 4 leaves, depending on size)

6 to 7 ripe passion fruits (see Note)

9 ounces bittersweet chocolate, roughly chopped

2 tablespoons (1 ounce) unsalted butter, at room temperature

1 tablespoon firmly packed light brown sugar

½ teaspoon vanilla extract

Pinch of kosher salt

2 tablespoons Dutch-process cocoa powder

BRIGHT AND FRESH

NOTE: Passion fruits are ripe and ready to eat once their smooth purple skin turns wrinkled.

STORE: The truffles can be stored in an airtight container in the refrigerator for up to 1 week. Layer the truffles between pieces of parchment so they don't stick together.

Line a baking tray with parchment paper. Lift the chilled truffle out of the loaf pan using the foil overhangs. Turn the truffle slab out onto a cutting board and remove the foil. Sift 1 tablespoon of the cocoa powder evenly over the truffle, then turn it over and dust the other side with the remaining 1 tablespoon of cocoa powder. Trim ¼ inch off each side of the truffle slab and cut the slab into 32 one-inch squares. (To get clean cuts, keep a tall glass of hot water nearby. Dip the knife into the water and wipe it dry before each cut.) Place the truffles on the prepared tray, cover in plastic wrap, and refrigerate until serving.

My amma's kulfi was my favorite childhood treat. Hers was a classic version, flavored with cardamom and ground pistachios. I have wonderful memories of playing in the hot sun with this cool, milky treat melting down my arm. My version of this common South Asian frozen dessert is made with homemade condensed milk, which gives the kulfi a creamy and pleasingly chewy texture. I add lemongrass to the milk for a lemony and deeply floral flavor and vanilla bean for sweet richness. This kulfi is made in a loaf pan. Served with fresh fruit like summer stone fruits or berries to cut through the richness, this is an impressive (and easy) plated dessert. But you could make Popsicles, too; they are better to eat while playing outside.

Lemongrass Kulfi

ACTIVE TIME: 10 minutes
TOTAL TIME: 4 hours, 30 minutes

Serves 10

3 fresh lemongrass stalks

1 vanilla bean

¾ cup granulated sugar

1 tablespoon finely grated lime zest

6 cups heavy cream

3¾ cups whole milk

¼ teaspoon kosher salt

Mango slices, raspberries, blackberries, or passion fruit, for garnish

TRIM AND PEEL THE LEMONGRASS STALKS AND CUT INTO 2-inch pieces. Bash them with a pestle or the handle of a large chef's knife to release more flavor. Slice the vanilla bean lengthwise and scrape out the seeds, retaining the pod. Combine the lemongrass, sugar, lime zest, cream, milk, and vanilla seeds and pod in a large saucepan over medium-high heat. Bring the mixture to a boil, then reduce the heat to low. Simmer until the mixture is reduced to a little less than 3 cups, about 2 to 2½ hours, stirring occasionally.

Coat a 1½-quart loaf pan with cooking spray, then line with plastic wrap. Once the mixture has reduced, stir in the salt. Strain the mixture through a fine-mesh sieve into a medium bowl and discard the solids. Pour the liquid into the prepared pan and freeze until firm, at least 4 hours.

To serve, turn the kulfi out of the pan and onto a serving platter. Cut into 10 slices, about ¾ inch thick each. This is a rich dessert—a little goes a long way. Cut each slice into 6 squares and place on a plate or pile up in a glass. Top with fresh fruit.

MAKE AHEAD: This is best made 1 day in advance.

STORE: Store in the freezer for up to 1 week.

Sumac is like a better lemon. It is bright, sour, and fruity, with less tartness than a lemon and more complexity. Because lemon pairs so well with blueberries, I had to try blueberries with sumac, even though it's usually thought of as a savory spice. The combination is absolutely scrumptious. In the filling for these handpies, the sumac gives the blueberries a citrusy zing and an underlying woodsy note. Mixed with sugar and sprinkled on the outside of the handpies, the slightly purple sumac is as beautiful as it is tasty.

Handpie Dough

IN A FOOD PROCESSOR, COMBINE THE FLOUR, SUGAR, baking powder, baking soda, and salt. Add the cubed butter and pulse until the butter is pea-sized. Transfer to a medium bowl and add ¾ cup of the buttermilk. Stir with a fork until the dough comes together when pressed. Add the remaining tablespoon of buttermilk if the dough is too dry. Transfer the dough to a lightly floured surface and knead a few times until it comes together. Roll the dough into a log approximately 12 inches long. Wrap in plastic wrap and chill for at least 2 hours or overnight.

Blueberry-Sumac Filling

IN A MEDIUM SAUCEPAN OVER MEDIUM HEAT, COMBINE blueberries, sugar, lemon juice, cornstarch, and salt. Bring to a simmer, stirring occasionally, and cook until the blueberries soften, about 5 minutes. With a slotted spoon, remove the blueberries to a medium bowl. Set aside. Continue to cook the sauce until slightly thickened, about 5 more minutes. Remove the pan from the heat. Stir in the reserved blueberries and the sumac. Chill in the refrigerator until the filling is cold, about 40 minutes.

(Continued)

Flaky Blueberry Handpies

ACTIVE TIME: 35 minutes
TOTAL TIME: 3 hours, 30 minutes

Makes 16 handpies

HANDPIE DOUGH

2 cups all-purpose flour

1 cup granulated sugar

1 teaspoon baking powder

¼ teaspoon baking soda

¾ teaspoon kosher salt

4 tablespoons (2 ounces)
cold unsalted butter, cut into cubes

¾ cup plus 1 tablespoon
cold buttermilk

BLUEBERRY-SUMAC FILLING

3 cups blueberries

¼ cup plus 2 tablespoons
granulated sugar

1 tablespoon freshly squeezed
lemon juice

1 tablespoon cornstarch

¼ teaspoon kosher salt

1 teaspoon sumac

(Continued)

ASSEMBLING THE HANDPIES

1 cup granulated sugar

1 teaspoon sumac

1 large egg

1 teaspoon water

Pinch of kosher salt

Peanut oil, for frying

SPECIAL EQUIPMENT

Deep-fry/candy thermometer (optional)

IN A SMALL BOWL, WHISK TOGETHER THE SUGAR AND sumac. In a separate small bowl, prepare an egg wash by whisking the egg with the water and salt. Remove the dough from the refrigerator and cut into 16 equal pieces. (Tip: Cut the cylinder in half, then cut each piece in half and so on to easily create equal-sized pieces.) Keeping the pieces of dough covered and chilled on a large plate or small tray, layered between parchment paper, take out three pieces at a time and roll into 4½-inch circles, dusting your work surface with a little flour if necessary to keep the dough from sticking.

Working with three chilled dough rounds at a time, brush the egg wash around the edge of the dough and place 1 tablespoon of blueberry-sumac filling in the middle. Fold the dough in half and crimp the edges closed with a fork. Repeat with the remaining dough rounds.

Lay some paper towels on a baking tray and place a cooling rack over it. Pour oil into a large, heavy-bottomed saucepan to a depth of 2 to 3 inches. Heat the oil to 350°F. Deep fry the pies, 2 or 3 at a time, until a deep golden brown, about 1 minute on each side. Transfer to the cooling rack to drain. Toss each pie in the sumac-sugar mixture while still hot. Fry and coat all the pies, being sure to maintain the oil at 350°F. Once all the pies are coated in sugar, serve immediately.

My eldest nephew, Averroes, loves sweet, sticky jam. He used to call me every month to ask me to pick up a particular strawberry-rhubarb jam from a bakery near my house. I dreamed up this recipe with Averroes in mind: strawberry jam with *flor de Jamaica*, the jewel-toned, lemony tart hibiscus flower. This jam is sweet but tangy, with a deep berry flavor, and because it doesn't have added pectin, it has a loose consistency. I was right: Averroes loved it, especially with a hot, crusty piece of buttered baguette. My strawberry hibiscus jam is his new monthly request.

SLICE OFF THE TOPS OF THE STRAWBERRIES AND CUT the berries in half. Slice the vanilla bean lengthwise and scrape out the seeds. Set aside the pod for later use.

In a medium bowl, combine the sugar, vanilla bean seeds, and lime zest. Rub the mixture between your fingers to evenly distribute and release the lime oils. The sugar will be slightly damp, sandy, and fragrant. Add most of the strawberries, reserving 2 cups for later use. Add the lime juice and toss the mixture until the strawberries are coated in sugar. Let sit at room temperature until the strawberries have released a significant amount of juice, about 30 minutes.

In a small bowl, crush the hibiscus into small pieces with your hands. Pour the boiling water over the hibiscus and allow to steep for 10 minutes. Strain the infusion through a fine-mesh sieve into another small bowl, making sure to squeeze out every last bit of liquid. Discard the petals.

In a large saucepan, combine the strawberry-sugar mixture, vanilla bean pod, and hibiscus water. Bring to a boil over medium-high heat, then reduce heat to medium-low and simmer, stirring occasionally, until the mixture is thick enough to coat the back of a spoon, about 25 minutes. Add the reserved 2 cups of strawberries. These berries will release liquid and the jam will thin out. Continue cooking

(Continued)

A's Strawberry Hibiscus Jam

ACTIVE TIME: 20 minutes
TOTAL TIME: 1 hour, 20 minutes

Makes 2½ cups

2 pounds strawberries

1 vanilla bean

1½ cups granulated sugar

2 teaspoons finely grated lime zest

2 tablespoons freshly squeezed lime juice

Scant 1 cup dried hibiscus flowers

¾ cup boiling water

SPECIAL EQUIPMENT

Deep-fry/candy thermometer (optional)

NOTE: You can also test the jam's consistency without a thermometer: Chill a small plate in the freezer until very cold, about 5 minutes. Spoon a little bit of jam onto the chilled plate and wait 2 to 3 minutes. Nudge the puddle of jam with the edge of a spoon. If it wrinkles a bit and appears thickened, it's done.

STORE: Spoon into jars and keep refrigerated for up to 2 months.

until a candy thermometer registers 215°F, another 20 to 25 minutes. Pour the hot jam into a bowl and press plastic wrap directly onto the surface of the jam to prevent it from forming a skin. Once the jam has cooled completely, remove the vanilla bean pod.

Chocolate Juniper Doughnuts

ACTIVE TIME: 40 minutes
TOTAL TIME: 1 hour

Makes 2 dozen doughnuts
plus doughnut holes

DOUGHNUTS

2 teaspoons juniper berries

2½ cups all-purpose flour,
plus extra for rolling the dough

½ cup malted milk powder

1 cup Dutch-process cocoa powder

2 teaspoons baking powder

1 teaspoon kosher salt

4 large eggs, at room temperature

1½ cups granulated sugar

⅓ cup buttermilk, at room temperature

5 tablespoons (2½ ounces)
unsalted butter, melted

4 cups peanut oil, plus more as needed

CHOCOLATE GLAZE

3 ounces unsweetened chocolate,
roughly chopped

¼ cup heavy cream

2 tablespoons water

1 teaspoon espresso powder

2 cups confectioners' sugar, sifted

(Continued)

Chocolate is rich, robust, and complex—but it's also a bit of a blank canvas for bakers. Because chocolate is bold and not easily overwhelmed by other flavors, it is the perfect foil for many spices, like juniper berries. Juniper berries are usually used with game meats or hearty stews (or gin, which gets its signature taste from juniper berries). Paired with chocolate, the clean, fresh evergreen flavor of juniper berries adds an unexpected note of sharp, sweet resin to these decadent doughnuts.

Doughnuts

IN A SKILLET OVER MEDIUM HEAT, TOAST THE JUNIPER berries until very fragrant, about 3 minutes. Grind the berries to a fine powder in a coffee grinder and measure out 1¼ teaspoons of juniper powder. Discard the rest or set aside for another use.

In a large bowl, sift together the flour, malted milk powder, cocoa powder, baking powder, salt, and the 1¼ teaspoons of juniper powder. In a medium bowl, whisk together the eggs, sugar, buttermilk, and butter until incorporated. Pour the egg mixture into the flour mixture and stir with a spatula until just combined. Allow the dough to rest in the refrigerator for 15 minutes.

Generously flour your work surface. This dough will be wet and sticky. Turn out the dough onto your work surface and lightly sprinkle flour on top of the dough as well. Pat or roll the dough to a thickness of ½ inch. Use the doughnut cutter dipped in flour to punch out doughnuts and doughnut holes. Gather up the scraps, reroll or pat the dough, and punch out more doughnuts and doughnut holes until all the dough has been used.

(Continued)

In a large, heavy-bottomed saucepan, heat the 4 cups of oil to 365°F. (The oil should always be 1½ to 2 inches deep. Add more oil as needed.) Cover a cooling rack with paper towels. Using a pastry brush, dust any excess flour off 1 doughnut, then carefully drop it into the oil. Do the same with 1 doughnut hole. These are your test doughnuts to check the frying time. Fry the doughnut hole for 30 seconds on each side; fry the whole doughnut for 1 minute on each side. Using tongs, remove the doughnuts from the oil and place on the paper towels to drain. Taste both doughnuts and adjust the frying time as needed. Working in batches, fry the remaining doughnuts.

Chocolate Glaze

PLACE THE CHOCOLATE IN A MEDIUM BOWL. IN A SMALL saucepan over medium heat, bring the cream, water, and espresso powder to a simmer. Pour the hot cream mixture over the chocolate. Let stand for 2 minutes, allowing the heat from the cream mixture to melt the chocolate. Add the sugar and whisk until smooth.

To put it all together

ONCE COOLED COMPLETELY, DIP THE DOUGHNUTS IN THE warm chocolate glaze and place on a tray to rest until cooled and set. Doughnuts are best the day they are made.

These light, airy meringues—created by my friend and fellow pastry chef Pichet Ong—are always a welcome end to a meal. Pichet is an expert in Asian flavors and often uses spice in his desserts. When I asked him to share a recipe for this book, he graciously offered me this inventive dish that shows off kaffir lime leaves. Their fresh, distinctive lemon-lime aroma is an intriguing addition to the lush tropical decadence of ripe mangoes.

Meringues

PREHEAT THE OVEN TO 200°F. LINE A BAKING TRAY WITH parchment paper.

Microwave the kaffir lime leaves for 10 seconds. Toss the leaves and repeat the process until they are dry and brittle, 10 to 12 more times. (I know this sounds like a lot, but trust me: it works.) In a coffee grinder, grind the leaves into a fine powder. Remove any stems that remain.

In the bowl of a stand mixer fitted with a whisk attachment, whip the egg whites, cream of tartar, and salt on medium speed until frothy. Gradually add the granulated sugar and increase speed to high, continuing to whip until firm peaks form. In a small bowl, sift together ¾ teaspoon of the lime leaf powder and the confectioners' sugar. Fold the confectioners' sugar mixture gently into the egg white mixture. Spoon the mixture onto the prepared baking tray to form 6 mounds. Use the back of a spoon to spread each mound into a round meringue about 4 inches wide with a slight indentation in the middle. Sprinkle another ¼ teaspoon of the lime leaf powder over the meringues. (Reserve another ½ teaspoon of the lime leaf powder for use in the macerated mangoes. Set aside any extra for another use.) Bake the meringues for 1 hour and 15 minutes. Allow to cool completely in the pan.

(Continued)

Mango and Cream Meringue Cakes

ACTIVE TIME: 30 minutes
TOTAL TIME: 1 hour, 45 minutes

Serves 6

MERINGUES

20 medium-sized fresh
kaffir lime leaves

Whites from 2 large eggs,
at room temperature

⅛ teaspoon cream of tartar

½ teaspoon kosher salt

½ cup granulated sugar

⅓ cup confectioners' sugar, sifted

MACERATED MANGOES

2 ripe mangoes,
such as Kent or Haitian

2 tablespoons granulated sugar

⅛ teaspoon kosher salt

1 tablespoon freshly squeezed
lemon juice

1½ teaspoons finely grated lemon zest

½ teaspoon lime leaf powder
(reserved from the meringue cakes)

2 tablespoons toasted unsweetened
finely shredded or desiccated coconut

(Continued)

BRIGHT AND FRESH

ASSEMBLING THE MERINGUE CAKES

1 cup heavy cream

Confectioners' sugar, for garnish

Macerated Mangoes

PEEL AND PIT THE MANGOES AND CUT THE FLESH INTO ½-inch pieces. In a medium bowl, stir together the mangoes, sugar, salt, lemon juice, lemon zest, lime leaf powder, and coconut. Let sit to macerate, about 2 hours.

Assembling the Meringue Cakes

IN A STAND MIXER FITTED WITH A WHISK ATTACHMENT, whip the cream until medium peaks form. Place each meringue in a serving dish. Dollop whipped cream in the indentation and top with one sixth of the macerated mangoes. Dust with confectioners' sugar and serve immediately.

MAKE AHEAD: Cooled meringues can be stored in an airtight container in the freezer for up to 2 weeks. Let them thaw for several hours before assembling and serving.

ON ONE AMAZING TRIP TO PARIS, I ATE AT GUY SAVOY, ONE OF THE world's most celebrated French restaurants. At the end of the meal the cheese course came. It included an apricot–cumin compote. It was sweet and tart, with the faintest hint of smoky, crushed cumin seeds. Until that moment, I thought I knew what cumin tasted like. Guy Savoy's pairing led me to discover a whole new side of a familiar spice. Stop and reconsider all the savory, earthy, and nutty spices in your pantry; there's magic awaiting on your spice rack.

Savory, Earthy, and Nutty

Apricot Almond Financiers

ACTIVE TIME: 15 minutes
TOTAL TIME: 45 minutes

Makes 2 dozen financiers

¾ teaspoon cumin seeds

8 tablespoons (4 ounces) unsalted butter

1¼ cups confectioners' sugar, plus more for garnish

½ cup natural almond flour (blanched is a fine substitute)

¼ cup plus 1 tablespoon all-purpose flour

½ teaspoon kosher salt

Whites from 4 large eggs, at room temperature

1 tablespoon mild olive oil

4 medium apricots, cut into ¼-inch dice

Cumin may be the world's most used spice. You'll taste it in dishes from India to North Africa to Mexico and, of course, in the Pakistani dishes I grew up with. But you might not recognize it in a dessert. Cumin adds finesse to these financiers and a touch of its enigmatic musk flavor. Studded with buttery apricots, this is a dessert you will not soon forget, I promise.

PREHEAT THE OVEN TO 375°F. BUTTER AND FLOUR A MINI muffin pan and place in the freezer until needed.

Toast the cumin seeds in a skillet over medium heat until fragrant, about 2 minutes. Use a mortar and pestle to coarsely grind the toasted cumin.

In a small saucepan over medium-high heat, melt the butter. Continue cooking until the solids turn brown and the butter begins to smell nutty, about 2½ minutes. The butter will be deep brown. Transfer to a small bowl to cool, being sure to scrape all the browned bits.

Into the bowl of a standing mixer fitted with a whisk attachment, sift together the confectioners' sugar, almond flour, all-purpose flour, salt, and cumin. Add the egg whites and beat on low speed until incorporated. Scrape down the sides of the bowl and mix again briefly. With the mixer running, drizzle in the browned butter (including the browned milk solids) and olive oil. Beat until the batter is smooth and emulsified.

Fill the muffin cups two-thirds full of batter. Top each with 3 pieces of the diced apricot. Sift a heavy layer of confectioners' sugar over each. Bake on the middle rack of the oven for 15 to 20 minutes, until golden brown. Let the financiers cool in the pan for 5 minutes, then transfer to a cooling rack. Allow to cool completely.

MAKE AHEAD: The batter can be made ahead of time and stored in the refrigerator for up to 2 days.

STORE: Financiers are best the day they are made, but if tightly wrapped, they can be stored at room temperature for up to 2 days.

In the Middle East, guests are traditionally welcomed with a light, aromatic spiced coffee called *gahwa*, which is served in a small cup alongside sweet dates. The coffee and the dates pair wondrously, balancing sweetness and bitterness. The spiced espresso-date filling in these bars does the same thing, while the semolina and unhulled sesame seeds add a deep, nutty flavor and a pleasantly crunchy, sandy texture to the crust.

Sesame Semolina Date Bars

ACTIVE TIME: 35 minutes
TOTAL TIME: 1 hour, 10 minutes

Makes 2 dozen bars

Sesame Semolina Dough

GREASE AN 8-INCH SQUARE PAN AND LINE WITH 2 CRISS-crossed pieces of parchment paper, creating a 1-inch overhang on all sides.

In a skillet over medium heat, toast the sesame seeds until fragrant, 2 to 3 minutes. In a large bowl, whisk together the toasted sesame seeds, flour, semolina, baking powder, salt, and sugar. In a small bowl, combine the espresso powder, water, and vanilla. In a medium saucepan over low heat, melt the butter and stir in the espresso mixture. Add the butter-espresso mixture to the flour mixture and stir until combined. Pat two-thirds of this dough into the prepared pan, pressing firmly. Stir the almonds into the remaining dough. Chill the pan of dough and the remaining dough in the refrigerator for about 20 minutes.

Date Filling

IN A SMALL SAUCEPAN OVER MEDIUM-HIGH HEAT, combine the dates and the water, cloves, ginger, cinnamon, salt, sugar, and orange juice and stir. Bring to a boil. Reduce the heat to low, cover, and simmer until the dates are tender and starting to break apart and the mixture thickens, 8 to 10 minutes. (Check occasionally to make sure the mixture isn't scorching on the bottom of the pan.) Remove the cover, stir in the orange zest, and continue to simmer, uncovered, for 2 minutes. The mixture should be a thick paste. Allow to cool completely.

SESAME SEMOLINA DOUGH

2 tablespoons unhulled sesame seeds

1¾ cups all-purpose flour

½ cup fine semolina (not semolina flour, see In Your Pantry, page 8)

1½ teaspoons baking powder

½ teaspoon kosher salt

¼ cup plus 2 tablespoons granulated sugar

1 tablespoon plus 1 teaspoon espresso powder

1 tablespoon hot water

1 teaspoon vanilla extract

11 tablespoons (5½ ounces) unsalted butter

¼ cup sliced almonds with skin (or blanched)

DATE FILLING

1¼ cups medjool dates, firmly packed, pitted and roughly chopped

1 cup water

Heaping ¼ teaspoon ground cloves

Heaping ¼ teaspoon ground ginger

(Continued)

(Continued)

Heaping ¼ teaspoon ground Vietnamese cinnamon

Heaping ¼ teaspoon kosher salt

1 tablespoon granulated sugar

3 tablespoons freshly squeezed orange juice

1¼ teaspoons finely grated orange zest

2 tablespoons confectioners' sugar, for garnish

To put it all together

POSITION AN OVEN RACK IN THE LOWER THIRD OF THE oven. Preheat the oven to 375°F. Using an offset spatula, spread the date filling evenly over the chilled dough in the pan. Crumble the reserved dough with almonds into big pieces over the filling. Bake for 30 to 35 minutes, until the top is browned and the almonds are golden. Let cool completely. Use the parchment overhang to remove the cooled dessert from the pan. Cut the slab into 8 long strips, then cut each strip into 3 rectangles to make 24 bars. Dust lightly with the confectioners' sugar.

MAKE AHEAD: The date filling can be made up to 2 days in advance and stored in the refrigerator.

Schiacciata con l'uva is a rustic flatbread enriched with olive oil and studded with grapes that is traditionally served as a snack in Tuscany. I had the delight of trying this bread during a fall visit to Italy. I vividly remember a large tray of it, bursting with juicy grapes, on the counter of a *pasticceria*. Sometimes you'll find an Italian recipe that calls for aniseseed, which I've used here, but my secret is just a touch of nigella seed. The subtle spice is peppery and slightly bitter, with the pungency of thyme, and it balances the sweet and musky flavor of the grapes. I've also broken with tradition by using a mixture of grapes—Concord grapes would be great, too—and ricotta, which dots the golden bread with pockets of creaminess.

IN A SMALL BOWL, COMBINE THE YEAST WITH THE WARM milk and 1 teaspoon of the granulated sugar. Set aside until frothy, about 3 minutes.

In the bowl of a stand mixer fitted with a dough hook, combine the flour, remaining 2 tablespoons plus 2 teaspoons of granulated sugar, and the salt. Add the yeast mixture, warm water, and the egg and egg yolk and beat on medium speed until a smooth, stiff dough forms, about 3 minutes. Add the butter 1 tablespoon at a time, beating after each addition until fully incorporated, about 3 minutes. Continue to beat the dough on medium-high until it pulls away from the sides and bottom of the bowl. Turn the dough out onto a lightly floured surface and knead for 1 minute. Place the dough in a lightly oiled large bowl, cover with plastic wrap, and allow to rise until doubled in size, about 1 hour.

Preheat the oven to 350°F. In a small skillet over medium heat, toast the aniseseeds and nigella seeds until fragrant, about 2 minutes. Use a mortar and pestle to crush the toasted seeds. Transfer the seeds to a small bowl and stir in the turbinado sugar. In a medium bowl, crush 2 cups of the grapes with your hands or a potato masher. In a separate small bowl, stir together the lemon zest, lemon juice, and ricotta.

(Continued)

Roasted Grape Focaccia

ACTIVE TIME: 35 minutes
TOTAL TIME: 2 hours, 55 minutes

Serves 12

2¼ teaspoons (1 package) active dry yeast

⅓ cup whole milk, warm to the touch but not hot, about 105°F

3 tablespoons granulated sugar, divided

2½ cups all-purpose flour

¾ teaspoons kosher salt

¼ cup warm water

1 large egg plus the yolk from 1 large egg, at room temperature

8 tablespoons (4 ounces) unsalted butter, at room temperature

1½ teaspoons aniseseeds

½ teaspoon nigella seeds

¼ cup plus 2 tablespoons turbinado sugar

4 cups (about 1¼ pounds) seedless black and red grapes, or Concord

½ teaspoon finely grated lemon zest

1 teaspoon freshly squeezed lemon juice

½ cup whole milk ricotta

2 tablespoons fruity extra-virgin olive oil, divided

¼ teaspoon fleur de sel

SAVORY, EARTHY, AND NUTTY

Oil a 9 × 13-inch pan with 1 tablespoon of the olive oil. Punch down the dough. Divide the risen dough into two unequal portions: the first portion will be about two-thirds of the dough, the second portion about one-third. Place the large portion in the oiled pan and gently stretch and press the dough to fill the pan. Evenly distribute about two-thirds of the crushed grapes and about half of the whole grapes over the dough. Spoon ricotta onto the dough in 9 evenly spaced dollops. Sprinkle with 3 tablespoons of the spiced turbinado sugar.

Lightly flour your work surface. Use a rolling pin to roll out the second, smaller portion of dough into a rectangle the size of the dough in the pan. Place the rolled-out dough on top of the first layer of dough and grapes. Brush the top with the remaining 1 tablespoon of olive oil. Evenly distribute the remaining one-third of the crushed grapes and the remaining whole grapes over the second layer of dough. Whisk the fleur de sel into the remaining spiced turbinado sugar and sprinkle on top of the dough.

Bake for 45 to 50 minutes, until both the bottom and the top of the bread are a rich golden brown. Cut into 12 pieces for serving.

STORE: The focaccia is best eaten the day it is made, but it can be stored in the fridge.

Apple Cheddar Caraway Scones

These scones are for my dear friend Meme, the scone expert. A little sweet, a little savory, and a little unexpected—these scones have it all. The rustic, sweet green flavor of caraway and the warm spice of paprika will definitely wake up your brunch. With toasty oat flour and intense dried apple, these scones are especially good with a spread of smoked salmon. Even better: the dough can be made in advance, which means you don't have to wake up early.

ACTIVE TIME: 30 minutes
TOTAL TIME: 1 hour, 10 minutes

 *Makes* 12 scones

1¼ cup all-purpose flour

½ cup oat flour

3 tablespoons granulated sugar

1½ teaspoons baking powder

1 teaspoon baking soda

1 teaspoon kosher salt, plus a pinch

8 tablespoons (4 ounces) cold unsalted butter, cut into ½-inch cubes

¾ teaspoon caraway seeds

1 cup dried apples, roughly chopped

²/₃ cup shredded sharp white cheddar cheese

¼ cup plus 2 tablespoons cold buttermilk

1 large egg, cold

2 teaspoons water

2 tablespoons turbinado sugar

½ teaspoon Hungarian sweet paprika or hot (depending on your preference)

½ teaspoon fleur de sel

SPECIAL EQUIPMENT

1½-inch ice cream scoop

IN A LARGE BOWL, WHISK TOGETHER THE ALL-PURPOSE flour, oat flour, granulated sugar, baking powder, baking soda, and 1 teaspoon of the salt. Add the butter, tossing to coat in the flour mixture. Chill in the freezer until very cold, about 15 minutes. When the butter is very cold, use your fingers or a pastry cutter to break it into small, pea-sized bits.

Use a mortar and pestle to crush the caraway seeds. Add the caraway seeds, dried apples, and shredded cheese to the flour mixture and toss to combine. Add the buttermilk and gently mix with your hands just until the dough begins to clump together. The texture will seem dry, almost like a pie dough. Line a baking tray with a nonstick baking mat or parchment paper. Using a 1½-inch ice cream scoop, scoop up portions of dough and deposit them, equally spaced 2 inches apart, on the prepared tray. Cover and refrigerate for 30 minutes.

Preheat the oven to 375°F.

In a small bowl, prepare an egg wash by whisking the egg with the water and a pinch of the salt. In a separate small bowl, combine the turbinado sugar, paprika, and fleur de sel. Brush the top of each scone lightly with egg wash. Sprinkle a heaping ½ teaspoon of the sugar-spice mixture over each scone. Bake for 18 to 20 minutes, until a wooden toothpick inserted into the center of a scone comes out clean.

MAKE AHEAD: You can freeze the scooped dough for up to 2 weeks. Defrost the frozen dough in the refrigerator overnight.

STORE: The scones are best eaten the day they are made, but if tightly wrapped, they can be stored at room temperature for 1 day.

I first created this recipe for an Ayurveda workshop to show how spices can be used to find balance in the body. I wasn't thinking too much about the balance of flavors, but the nuts turned out to be delicious. I tweaked the recipe just a little bit and found that they were a holiday hit. The spice blend is unusual and fragrant, with sweetness, warmth, and savor from the pimentón de la Vera, a type of smoked paprika, and cumin. They are great for snacking, for serving with cocktails, or for sprinkling on top of a salad. Plus, the egg white in the recipe gives the nuts a glossy sheen and a long shelf life, making them a perfect gift.

PREHEAT THE OVEN TO 300°F. LINE A BAKING TRAY WITH parchment paper and lightly grease with coconut oil.

Put the coconut palm sugar, granulated sugar, honey, egg white, 1 tablespoon of coconut oil, pimentón de la Vera, cumin, allspice, cinnamon, and salt into a medium bowl and whisk well to eliminate any lumps. Add the pecans and almonds and toss to coat evenly. Bake for 30 to 40 minutes, stirring occasionally, until roasted dark brown. The nuts will still appear wet when they are done; this coating will harden as it cools. Sprinkle the fleur de sel over the warm nuts and toss the nuts as they cool so they don't clump.

STORE: Store the nuts in an airtight container at room temperature for up to 2 weeks.

Honey Lacquered Nuts

ACTIVE TIME: 10 minutes
TOTAL TIME: 1 hour

Makes 4 cups

3 tablespoons coconut palm sugar

½ cup granulated sugar

¼ cup mild honey

White from 1 large egg

1 tablespoon coconut oil, melted, plus more for greasing (oil can be substituted)

½ teaspoon pimentón de la Vera (any smoked paprika is a fine substitute)

½ teaspoon ground cumin

Heaping ⅛ teaspoon freshly ground allspice

1 teaspoon ground Vietnamese cinnamon

½ teaspoon kosher salt

2 cups pecan halves

2 cups whole raw almonds with skin

1 teaspoon fleur de sel

Concord Grape Pie

ACTIVE TIME: 1 hour, 30 minutes
TOTAL TIME: 3 hours, 30 minutes

Serves 8

PIE DOUGH

2 teaspoons fennel seeds

¼ cup plus 2 tablespoons ice water

¼ teaspoon white vinegar

2 cups all-purpose flour

1 teaspoon granulated sugar

¼ teaspoon kosher salt

12 tablespoons (6 ounces) cold unsalted butter, cut into ½-inch cubes and stored in the freezer until ready to use

GRAPE FILLING

1½ pounds Concord grapes

½ cup plus 1 tablespoon granulated sugar

⅛ teaspoon kosher salt

2 tablespoons quick-cooking, granulated tapioca

BUTTERMILK GLAZE

½ cup confectioners' sugar

1 tablespoon buttermilk

¼ teaspoon vanilla extract

Pinch of kosher salt

(Continued)

When I was a kid, I was obsessed with grape juice. I was fascinated by its deep purple color and by its flavor. I would drink quarts, and my amma could never keep enough at home. I didn't actually taste a real Concord grape until years later, when amma brought some home from a local Asian grocery store. I got hooked on those, too, and would eat the whole flat in one sitting. Now, during fall's short Concord grape season, I cook and bake the sweet, tart fruit into everything I can think of: jams, sorbet, and—my favorite—pie. This pie has a slightly runny filling that reminds me of good old grape juice and a buttery, flaky dough dressed up with earthy fennel seeds. Finished with a tangy buttermilk glaze, this pie is so good you don't even need ice cream.

Pie Dough

IN A SKILLET OVER MEDIUM HEAT, TOAST THE FENNEL seeds until very fragrant and golden brown, 2 to 3 minutes. Let the seeds cool, then use a mortar and pestle to lightly crush them. In a small bowl, combine the water and vinegar.

In the bowl of a stand mixer fitted with a paddle attachment, mix the flour, sugar, salt, and crushed fennel seeds on low speed to combine. Add the butter and beat on medium speed until the butter is roughly the size of peas. Reduce the speed to low and add the vinegar mixture 1 tablespoon at a time, but stop the mixer and check the consistency of the dough before you have used it all. (You may not need all of the liquid, or you may need a little more.) The dough should hold together in your hand with no dry or crumbly bits, but it shouldn't form one large ball yet. If the dough is a bit dry after all the liquid has been added, add additional ice water a little at a time.

Turn the dough out onto the countertop and bring the dough together into a ball. Divide the dough into 2 uneven pieces: 1 piece should be one-third of the dough, for the top crust, and the other should be two-thirds, for the bottom crust. Lightly flour a sheet of parchment paper placed on your countertop. Place the smaller piece of dough on the parchment and roll into a 10-inch circle. Dust the dough

(Continued)

ASSEMBLING THE PIE

1 large egg

2 teaspoons water

Pinch of kosher salt

1 tablespoon unsalted butter,
at room temperature

with a little flour if it sticks to the rolling pin or parchment paper. With a small cutter cut out little circles or other shapes in the top-crust dough or create 4 or 5 slits with a sharp knife. Cover with a second sheet of parchment, transfer to a baking tray, and refrigerate.

Lightly flour another sheet of parchment paper and roll out the larger piece of dough into an 11- to 12-inch circle. Cover with a second sheet of parchment, transfer to another baking tray, and refrigerate.

Grape Filling

RINSE THE GRAPES AND POP THE FLESH FROM THE SKINS with your fingers, putting the pulp into a medium saucepan and the skins into a medium bowl. (This is tedious and a little messy, but stick with it.) Bring the pulp to a boil over medium-high heat and then reduce the heat to medium. Cook until the pulp has broken down, 8 to 10 minutes. Place a fine-mesh sieve over the bowl of grape skins. Use a rubber spatula to press the pulp through the sieve to remove the seeds. Discard the seeds. Combine the grape pulp and skins and let cool. Just before baking, stir in the sugar, salt, and tapioca.

Buttermilk Glaze

IN A SMALL BOWL, WHISK TOGETHER ALL THE INGREDIENTS until smooth. The mixture should be thick but runny. Transfer to a plastic food-storage bag and cut a small hole in one corner.

Assembling the Pie

POSITION AN OVEN RACK IN THE LOWER THIRD OF THE oven. Preheat the oven to 375°F. In a small bowl, prepare an egg wash by whisking the egg with the water and salt. Line a baking tray with parchment paper to catch any drips from the pie while it bakes.

Lightly dust your work surface with flour. Take the larger dough circle out of the freezer. Have a 9-inch pie pan ready. Roll the dough onto the rolling pin. Slide the pie pan under the dough and ease the dough onto the pan, unrolling the dough away from you and centering the circle on the pan. Gently press the dough to help it settle into the pan. Pour the grape filling into the dough-lined pan and dot with pieces of the butter. Remove the second, smaller dough circle from the freezer. By the same method, transfer the dough to the top of the pie, centering the circle over the pie. Gently press the top and bottom edges of the crust together. Brush the top of the pie with the egg wash and place the pie onto the prepared baking tray.

Bake for 40 minutes. Rotate the baking tray and reduce the heat to 350°F. Bake for an additional 45 to 50 minutes, until the crust is a deep, golden brown and the filling is bubbling. If the crust starts to get too dark before the pie is baked through, cover it with aluminum foil, either the whole crust or just the edges. Transfer the pie pan to a wire rack to cool.

When the pie has completely cooled, drizzle the buttermilk glaze over the top crust. Let the glaze harden, about 45 minutes, before serving.

MAKE AHEAD: The dough can be made up to 1 month ahead and stored in the freezer. Defrost the dough in the refrigerator overnight before using. For the filling, the grapes can be cooked and strained up to 2 days in advance, but wait to add the sugar, salt, and tapioca until just before assembling the pie.

STORE: This pie is best the day it's made, but tightly wrapped leftovers can be stored in the refrigerator for up to 2 days. Warm before serving.

SAVORY, EARTHY, AND NUTTY

Semolina is a much-loved ingredient in the Pakistani desserts I grew up with, but this cake is my take on a classic Lebanese semolina cake called *sfouf*, which is made with turmeric, a distinctly yellow spice with a noticeably earthy and slightly bitter flavor. Sfouf is very rich and moist, with a crispy exterior. The tahini that is brushed onto the pan creates that great crunch and a unique flavor. In this version, I add black sesame seeds to give the cake a more dominant sesame flavor, and the sesame seeds and the golden raisins also give the cake an appealing texture.

POSITION AN OVEN RACK IN THE MIDDLE OF THE OVEN. Preheat the oven to 375°F. Brush the tahini evenly onto the bottom and sides of each cup of a 12-cup muffin pan and place in the freezer.

In a small bowl, combine 2 tablespoons of the sugar, the sesame seeds, and ⅛ teaspoon of the salt. Remove the pan from the freezer and sprinkle each cup with the sesame sugar, making sure to coat the cups evenly. Return the pan to the freezer until needed.

In a small saucepan over medium heat, combine 2 tablespoons of the butter and the turmeric. Once the butter is melted, stir to combine and cook until foamy, about 1 minute. Add the remaining butter and reduce the heat to low. Heat until the butter is melted, then transfer the mixture to a medium bowl and allow to cool.

Into a large bowl, sift the semolina, flour, baking powder, the remaining ½ cup plus 2 tablespoons sugar, and the remaining ⅛ teaspoon of salt. When the butter is cool, add the milk, water, and vanilla and whisk together. Add this mixture to the semolina mixture and whisk until just combined and lump free. Stir in the golden raisins, if using.

Scoop ¼ cup of batter into each prepared muffin cup. Bake for 35 to 40 minutes, until golden brown, firm to the touch at the edge but just a bit soft in the center. Place the pan on a wire rack to cool for 10 minutes. Run a paring knife around the edges of the muffin cups to loosen the friands, then turn them out onto the wire rack to cool fully.

Golden Semolina Friands

ACTIVE TIME: 20 minutes
TOTAL TIME: 1 hour

Makes 12 friands

2 tablespoons cold tahini

¾ cup granulated sugar

2 teaspoons black sesame seeds

¼ teaspoon kosher salt

8 tablespoons (4 ounces)
unsalted butter

¼ teaspoon ground turmeric

1 cup fine semolina
(not semolina flour,
see In Your Pantry, page 8)

½ cup all-purpose flour

½ teaspoon baking powder

¾ cup whole milk

2 tablespoons water

¼ teaspoon vanilla extract

¼ cup golden raisins (optional)

STORE: The cake is best eaten the day it is made, but if tightly wrapped, it will keep well for 1 or 2 days at room temperature.

Gooey Cajeta Brownies

ACTIVE TIME: 45 minutes
TOTAL TIME: 3 hours

Makes 12 brownies

CAJETA

1 cup granulated sugar

2 tablespoons light corn syrup

¼ cup water

½ cup evaporated goat milk

¼ cup heavy cream

1 teaspoon kosher salt

BROWNIE BATTER

1¼ cups all-purpose flour

2 tablespoons Dutch-process cocoa

1 teaspoon kosher salt

11 ounces bittersweet chocolate, roughly chopped

16 tablespoons (2 sticks; 8 ounces) unsalted butter

5 large eggs, at room temperature

1 cup granulated sugar

1 cup firmly packed dark brown sugar

2 teaspoons espresso powder

1 teaspoon vanilla extract

GARNISH

¼ teaspoon fleur de sel

2 teaspoons coarse white sanding sugar or turbinado sugar

I know I had you at "gooey." I started making deliciously gooey *cajeta* when I worked at Balthazar Bakery in New York years ago. That's where I first got a taste for this unusual, pungent caramel made with goat's milk. Its one-of-a-kind flavor is a great match with a simple, deeply chocolate brownie. Where's the spice? It's the fleur de sel sprinkled there on the top, sparking your tastebuds and making everything taste a little better. This salted caramel brownie is my most requested item. Even customers who order a dozen tell me they don't always share.

Cajeta

IN A MEDIUM SAUCEPAN, COMBINE THE SUGAR, CORN syrup, and water. Brush the sides of the pan with a wet pastry brush to ensure there is no sugar stuck there, which can cause crystals to form in the cajeta. Cook over medium-high heat until the sugar is a medium amber color. Remove from the heat and whisk in the evaporated milk, cream, and salt. Be careful: the mixture will bubble furiously. Transfer the caramel to a medium bowl and chill in the freezer until very cold, about 1 hour.

Brownie Batter

SIFT TOGETHER THE FLOUR, COCOA, AND SALT INTO A medium bowl and whisk to combine. In a double boiler, melt the chopped chocolate and butter and stir to combine. Remove from the heat. In a separate double boiler or metal bowl over simmering water, whisk together the eggs, granulated sugar, brown sugar, and espresso powder. Whisk occasionally until the sugars have dissolved and the egg mixture is warm and no longer gritty, 2 to 3 minutes. Pour the chocolate mixture into the warm egg mixture, then add the vanilla and whisk well to combine. Use a rubber spatula to gently fold in the flour mixture until just combined with a few small streaks of flour remaining. (If you mix it too much, the brownies will lose their fudgy texture.)

(Continued)

To put it all together

PREHEAT THE OVEN TO 350°F. GREASE A 9 × 13-INCH PAN and line with a piece of parchment paper long enough to create a 1-inch overhang on two sides of the pan.

Pour half the brownie batter into the prepared pan and spread with an offset spatula to cover the bottom of the pan. Drizzle the batter with the chilled cajeta, leaving a 1-inch border uncovered so the cajeta won't ooze out during baking. Dollop the remaining brownie batter over the cajeta, covering as much of it as possible. Use an offset spatula to spread the batter evenly and fill in any holes.

Bake for 10 minutes. Remove the brownies from the oven and sprinkle with the fleur de sel and turbinado sugar. Gently pat down the topping with an offset spatula. Return the pan to the oven and bake for another 40 minutes or so, turning the pan halfway through baking, until a wooden toothpick inserted into the center comes out with a slightly damp crumb. Let the brownies cool for 15 minutes in the pan, then run a knife around the edges of the pan to loosen the brownies. Transfer the pan to the refrigerator to continue to cool until the brownies are firm, at least 2 hours.

Grip both of the parchment overhangs to remove the brownies from the pan. Turn the brownie slab upside down on a cutting board and use a serrated knife to trim about ½ inch from each side. Cut the rest into 12 equal pieces.

Kheer—or rice pudding—is the ultimate comfort food in any Pakistani household. The recipe is passed down from generation to generation, and each family has its own unique take on the basic combination of basmati rice and milk. Some are flavored with rose water, and others are studded with nuts or dates. My approach, of course, stars my amma's favorite spice: cardamom. This rice pudding—a *firni*, made with ground rice instead of whole rice grains—is simply spiced and served with a bold, fruity caramel made from tamarind pods native to North Africa. It is as unusual as it is tasty.

Rice Pudding

IN A SMALL BOWL, COMBINE THE BASMATI RICE WITH enough cold water to cover the rice by 2 inches. Soak for 30 minutes and drain through a sieve, reserving the rice. Pulse the soaked rice in a food processor to break the grains into small, uniform pieces.

In a large saucepan, combine the whole milk and the ground rice. On a cutting board, whack the cardamom pods with the blunt edge of a knife to crack them, then tie them up in cheesecloth and submerge the bundle in the milk mixture. Bring the mixture to a boil over medium-high heat, then reduce the heat to low and simmer, stirring frequently, until the milk has thickened and the rice is cooked, about 40 minutes.

Remove the pan from the heat, remove the cardamom pods, and stir in the cream, sweetened condensed milk, vanilla, and salt. Refrigerate until very cold, at least 3 hours and as long as overnight.

(Continued)

Creamy Firni with Tamarind Caramel

ACTIVE TIME: 1 hour
TOTAL TIME: 4 hours

Serves 6

RICE PUDDING

¼ cup basmati rice

6 cups whole milk

6 cardamom pods

½ cup heavy cream

¾ cup sweetened condensed milk

1 teaspoon vanilla extract

⅛ teaspoon kosher salt

TAMARIND CARAMEL

12 ounces tamarind pods

2¾ cups water, divided

1 cup granulated sugar

1 teaspoon light corn syrup

2 tablespoons (1 ounce) unsalted butter

Tamarind Caramel

FIRST, PREPARE THE TAMARIND: REMOVE THE HARD outer shell of the tamarind pods with you fingers, and remove as many of the sturdy fibers around the fruit as possible. In a small saucepan over medium-high heat, combine the tamarind fruit and 2 cups of the water. Bring to a boil, then reduce the heat to low and simmer until the pulp breaks down to form a paste with the water, 30 to 40 minutes. Remove from the heat and strain through a fine-mesh sieve over a medium bowl, and use a spatula to press through as much pulp as possible. Discard the seeds. You should have about ½ cup of pulp. Return the pulp to the saucepan and add the remaining ¾ cup of water. Cook over medium-high heat until the tamarind puree has reduced to 1 cup, 10 to 12 minutes.

In a medium saucepan over medium-high heat, cook the sugar and corn syrup until the sugar melts and caramelizes to a deep tan color, 4 to 5 minutes. Add the prepared tamarind puree and whisk to combine. Whisk in the butter. Remove from the heat and allow to cool to room temperature.

To put it all together

DIVIDE THE FIRNI INTO BOWLS AND DRIZZLE EACH SERVing with 2 tablespoons of the caramel. Store any leftover caramel in the refrigerator for another use, such as pouring over ice cream.

Strawberry– Spice Fruit Leather

I grew up eating Fruit Roll-Ups and absolutely loved them. They were the first thing I grabbed from the kitchen pantry when I got home from school. Now my kids ask for this easy and even more delicious homemade version to take to school as a treat for themselves and their friends. The balsamic vinegar in this recipe makes the strawberries taste more "red"—sweeter without being sugary—and the cubeb pepper dances on your tongue. There's only a little bit of this delicious pepper in the recipe, but that's what makes the final leather so good. Instead of being overwhelmed by the pepper, you are surprised by every little "pop" of heat.

ACTIVE TIME: 20 minutes
TOTAL TIME: Overnight

Makes 12 pieces

1 pound strawberries, hulled

¼ cup plus 2 tablespoons mild honey

1 teaspoon balsamic vinegar

Heaping ¼ teaspoon ground cubeb pepper

PREHEAT THE OVEN TO 200°F. LINE A BAKING TRAY WITH a nonstick baking mat.

Puree all the ingredients in a blender. Pour the puree onto the baking tray and use an offset spatula to spread it evenly to the edges of the pan. Bake for 3 to 5 hours, depending on the moisture content of the strawberries, until the fruit leather is nearly dry. (It's okay if the leather remains a little tacky; overdrying will make it hard.) Turn off the heat and continue to let the leather dry in the oven overnight.

Cut a piece of parchment paper slightly larger than the baking tray and place on the counter. Take the baking mat off the pan, and turn it upside down over the parchment. Gently pull the leather from the mat and release it onto the parchment paper. From the short side of the leather, very tightly roll up the fruit leather in the parchment. Using an oiled serrated knife, cut the roll of fruit leather into 12 pieces, each about 1 inch wide.

NOTE: If you can't find cubeb pepper, regular black pepper is a good substitute.

STORE: The fruit leather can be stored in an airtight container at room temperature for up to 1 week.

Best-Ever Honey-Glazed Corn Muffins

ACTIVE TIME: 20 minutes
TOTAL TIME: 40 minutes

Makes 12 muffins

The best cornbread I've ever had was at Spago when Sherry Yard was the executive pastry chef. It was moist and rich, and it was the one thing I always begged to take home with me. Sherry finally shared the recipe, and it has been a staple of our Thanksgiving table ever since. Because it is too good to make just once a year, it also shows up anytime we have fried chicken or chili, too. This is a spiced version of Sherry's cornbread. I added some smoke and heat to the glaze and some corn kernels to the batter for texture. You can amp it up even more by throwing some chopped cilantro or jalapeños in with the corn, or you can keep it simple. Either way, this is about to become your new go-to cornbread recipe.

CORN MUFFINS

4 tablespoons (2 ounces) unsalted butter, divided

¾ cup fresh corn kernels (frozen can be substituted)

1 teaspoon kosher salt, divided

½ cup yellow cornmeal

½ cup all-purpose flour

2 tablespoons cake flour

½ cup granulated sugar

1 tablespoon baking powder

2 large eggs, at room temperature

3 tablespoons grapeseed oil

½ cup whole milk, at room temperature

¼ cup buttermilk, at room temperature

(Continued)

Corn Muffins

PREHEAT THE OVEN TO 350°F. LINE A MUFFIN PAN WITH 12 paper liners.

In a skillet over medium-high heat, melt 1 tablespoon of the butter. Add the corn kernels and ¼ teaspoon of the salt and sauté until lightly cooked but still crunchy, about 5 minutes. Set aside.

In a medium bowl, sift together the cornmeal, all-purpose flour, cake flour, sugar, baking powder, and the remaining ¾ teaspoon of salt. Sift a second time. In a large bowl, whisk the eggs. In a small saucepan over medium heat, melt the remaining 3 tablespoons of butter and immediately drizzle the butter into the eggs, whisking continuously. Add the oil, milk, and buttermilk to the egg mixture and whisk to combine. Add the flour mixture and whisk until just combined. Fold in the sautéed corn.

Scoop about ¼ cup batter into each of the prepared muffin cups. Bake for 18 to 20 minutes, until a wooden toothpick inserted in the muffin comes out clean.

(Continued)

HONEY GLAZE

1 teaspoon cumin seeds

2 tablespoons (1 ounce)
unsalted butter

2 tablespoons mild honey

1 teaspoon water

¼ teaspoon pimentón de la Vera

⅛ teaspoon ground cayenne

Honey Glaze

WHILE THE MUFFINS ARE BAKING, MAKE THE HONEY glaze. Toast the cumin seeds in a skillet over medium heat until fragrant, about 2 minutes. Use a mortar and pestle to crush the toasted cumin. In a small saucepan over medium heat, melt the butter. Whisk in honey, water, toasted cumin, pimentón de la Vera, and cayenne.

When the muffins are done, prick the tops all over with a toothpick and brush each muffin generously with the glaze.

STORE: The glazed muffins can be stored in the refrigerator for up to 2 days. Warm them in a 350°F oven for 4 or 5 minutes to break the chill.

This pandowdy is a light, fresh, and fragrant take on a classic apple dessert. Usually you'd see warm spices like cinnamon and clove in a recipe like this, but those warm flavors can smother the sweet-tart taste of fresh, seasonal apples. This unusual blend of spices—slightly sweet, maple-like fenugreek, lightly floral mace, and bright black pepper—complements the apple flavor instead of masking it. Served warm, this is great with vanilla ice cream.

Apple Fenugreek Pandowdy

ACTIVE TIME: 40 minutes
TOTAL TIME: 2 hours, 30 minutes

Serves 8

Pandowdy Dough

IN THE BOWL OF A FOOD PROCESSOR, COMBINE THE flour, sugar, baking powder, and salt. Pulse several times to combine. Add the butter and pulse until it forms pea-sized chunks. Drizzle cold water over the flour mixture 1 tablespoon at a time, pulsing between additions, until the dough just beings to clump. (You may not need to use all the water. An overly wet dough will be tough and difficult to handle.) Pat the dough into a square, wrap in plastic wrap, and chill for at least 1 hour in the refrigerator.

Apple-Fenugreek Filling

PEEL, CORE, AND QUARTER THE APPLES. CUT EACH quarter into ½-inch slices. In a large bowl, whisk together the maple sugar, maple syrup, lemon juice, fenugreek, mace, black pepper, and salt. Toss the apples in the mixture to coat. Allow the apples to marinate for at least 30 minutes.

In a small saucepan, cook the butter over medium-high heat until the milk solids are medium brown and the butter smells toasty, about 3 minutes. Pour the browned butter over the apple mixture. In a small bowl, whisk the apple cider and cornstarch until the cornstarch is dissolved. Pour the cornstarch mixture over the apple mixture and stir.

(Continued)

PANDOWDY DOUGH

¾ cup all-purpose flour

1 tablespoon granulated sugar

¾ teaspoon baking powder

¾ teaspoon kosher salt

9 tablespoons (4½ ounces) cold unsalted butter, cut into ½-inch cubes

3 tablespoons ice water

APPLE-FENUGREEK FILLING

3 pounds firm, sweet apples, such as Honey Crisp, Pink Lady, or Mutsu

¼ cup maple sugar

¼ cup pure Grade B maple syrup

2 tablespoons freshly squeezed lemon juice

2½ teaspoons ground fenugreek

¼ teaspoon ground mace

Scant ¼ teaspoon freshly ground black pepper

½ teaspoon kosher salt

(Continued)

SAVORY, EARTHY, AND NUTTY

To put it all together

PREHEAT THE OVEN TO 400°F. TRANSFER THE APPLE-
fenugreek filling to a 12-inch cast iron skillet.

Flour your work surface well. Using a rolling pin, roll out
the pandowdy dough into a 12-inch square. Cut the square
into 4 smaller squares. Cut 2 of those squares diagonally to
form 4 large triangles, and cut the remaining 2 squares on
both diagonals to form a total of 8 smaller triangles. You
will have a total of 12 triangles of various sizes, which you
will use to make a top crust. (This is just a general guide on
cutting; you can cut a variety of triangles out of the 12-inch
square.) Return the dough to the refrigerator on a lined baking tray or a plate until firm, about 7 minutes. Once chilled,
overlap the triangles on top of the filling in the skillet and
brush the top with cream. Sprinkle with the maple sugar.

Bake for 15 minutes to caramelize the maple sugar.
Reduce the oven temperature to 375°F and bake for 25 to 30
more minutes more, until the apples are fork tender and the
juices are bubbling. Serve warm.

STORE: The pandowdy can be stored in the refrigerator for up
to 2 days. Warm it in the oven at 350°F for about 10 minutes
before serving.

3 tablespoons (1½ ounces)
unsalted butter

2 tablespoons apple cider or juice

2 tablespoons cornstarch

TOPPING

2 tablespoons heavy cream

2 tablespoons maple sugar

Everybody knows that chocolate and nuts go well together, so why not chocolate and sesame seeds? Unhulled sesame seeds have a pronounced nuttiness, and the tiny tear-shaped seeds give an unexpected texture to baked goods. Sesame seeds are the over-the-top touch in the ultimate sweet-savory streusel that crowns these rich chocolate muffins—the macadamia nuts have a buttery, almost creamy texture, the fleur de sel gives that hint of saltiness, and the sesame seeds add an addictive, nutty crunch.

PREHEAT THE OVEN TO 350°F. GREASE 18 CUPS OF TWO muffin pans with olive oil or cooking spray.

In a small skillet over medium heat, toast the sesame seeds until fragrant, 1 to 2 minutes.

In a medium bowl, whisk together ¾ cup of the flour and the light brown sugar and fleur de sel. Add the butter, nuts, and toasted sesame seeds and stir to form a chunky streusel. Refrigerate while you make the muffin batter.

To make the muffin batter, in a large bowl, whisk together the remaining 1¾ cup flour and the granulated sugar, baking soda, baking powder, cocoa powder, and salt. In a food processor or using a fork, puree or mash the bananas. Measure out 1¼ cups of banana puree and discard any extra or set aside for another use. In a medium bowl, whisk together the banana puree, eggs, and olive oil. Pour the banana mixture into the flour mixture and stir until just combined. Fold in the chopped chocolate.

Scoop ⅓ cup of batter into each prepared muffin cup, filling it approximately two-thirds full. Top each with 1 heaping tablespoon of the chilled streusel, then divide any leftover streusel evenly among the muffins. Bake for 15 to 18 minutes, until a wooden toothpick inserted into the center of a muffin comes out clean. Let cool completely in the pan before serving.

STORE: Store in an airtight container at room temperature for up to 2 days.

Dark Cocoa Banana Muffins with Salty Macadamia Streusel

ACTIVE TIME: 30 minutes
TOTAL TIME: 50 minutes

Makes 18 muffins

2 tablespoons unhulled sesame seeds

2½ cups all-purpose flour, divided

½ cup plus 2 tablespoons firmly packed light brown sugar

1½ teaspoons fleur de sel

6 tablespoons (3 ounces) unsalted butter, melted

½ cup roasted, unsalted macadamia nuts, roughly chopped

1½ cups plus 1 tablespoon granulated sugar

1 teaspoon baking soda

½ teaspoon baking powder

½ cup Dutch-process cocoa powder

¼ teaspoon kosher salt

2 or 3 very ripe bananas

3 large eggs, at room temperature

½ cup plus 2 tablespoons mild olive oil

9 ounces milk chocolate, roughly chopped

Toasted Brown Butter Matcha Crispies

ACTIVE TIME: 25 minutes
TOTAL TIME: 1 hour, 10 minutes

Makes 2 dozen pieces

CRISPIE BARS

1½ cups unsweetened coconut chips or flakes

4½ cups brown rice cereal

4 tablespoons (2 ounces) unsalted butter

10 ounces marshmallows

WHITE CHOCOLATE MATCHA COATING

16 ounces white chocolate, roughly chopped

1 tablespoon coconut oil

2 tablespoons plus 2 teaspoons matcha

⅛ teaspoon kosher salt

½ cup freeze-dried strawberries, finely chopped, for topping

Matcha is a ceremonial Japanese green tea that neither looks nor tastes like any tea you've ever had. The tea has been ground into a fine powder that resembles bright green cocoa, and the flavor is very vegetal, with a lingering sweetness and a slight, pleasant bitterness. I was introduced to the flavor of matcha on a trip to Japan. It was served at the end of many meals and was an ingredient in everything from croissants to ice cream. Matcha also works especially well with chocolate, making it even more complex. Look for a cooking-grade matcha, not an expensive ceremonial grade, which is best for drinking.

Crispie Bars

PREHEAT THE OVEN TO 300°F. IN A 9 × 13-INCH PAN, toast the coconut until golden, 6 to 8 minutes. Allow to cool completely. Transfer to a large bowl and stir in the brown rice cereal. Grease the same 9 × 13-inch pan.

In a medium saucepan over medium heat, melt the butter and continue to cook until the solids start to brown, about 3 minutes. Add the marshmallows and cook, stirring occasionally, until the marshmallows have completely melted and the butter is incorporated. Add the hot marshmallow mixture to the rice cereal mixture and stir vigorously with a rubber spatula until the cereal is evenly coated. Transfer the mixture into the prepared pan. Rub a little bit of butter on your hands and firmly press the mixture into the pan so that it is flat and firmly and evenly packed. Let cool until set, about 30 minutes.

Run a sharp knife around the edges of the pan to loosen the crispie slab, then turn it out onto a cutting board. Using a serrated knife, trim ½ inch off each edge, then cut the rectangle lengthwise into 2 strips about 4 inches wide. Next, cut each strip into 1-inch pieces to make 24 long rectangles.

(Continued)

White Chocolate Matcha Coating

IN A DOUBLE BOILER, MELT THE WHITE CHOCOLATE AND coconut oil and stir to combine. Add the matcha and salt and stir until the matcha is completely dissolved.

To put it all together

LINE A BAKING TRAY WITH PARCHMENT PAPER. DIP EACH crispie bar halfway into the white chocolate matcha coating. Lay the dipped bars on the parchment paper and sprinkle the strawberries over the chocolate, evenly distributing it among the bars. Refrigerate for 15 minutes to set. (If left in the refrigerator any longer, the strawberries will absorb moisture and lose their crunch.)

MAKE AHEAD: You can make the crispie bars up to 2 days in advance, but don't dip them in chocolate more than 1 day in advance or the strawberries will get soggy.

STORE: Store in an airtight container at room temperature for up to 3 days.

Apricot–Rosemary Coins

ACTIVE TIME: 20 minutes
TOTAL TIME: 1 hour

Makes 3 dozen cookies

1 cup water

4 ounces dried apricots

1¾ cups all-purpose flour

1 cup fine cornmeal

1 teaspoon baking soda

¾ teaspoon kosher salt

1¼ cups granulated sugar

1 teaspoon finely grated orange zest

16 tablespoons (2 sticks; 8 ounces) unsalted butter, at room temperature

2 teaspoons finely chopped fresh rosemary leaves

1 teaspoon vanilla extract

2 large eggs, at room temperature

What I like best about this cookie is the reaction people have when they first taste it. It looks simple, but the flavor is a surprise. No one expects the rosemary. Its assertive, piney fragrance jump-starts your palate while the nutty cornmeal is comfortable and familiar. Watching people react to the unexpected flavor combination—seeing their excitement and their effort to put into words their enthusiasm for it, that expression of joy—is the reason I cook.

PREHEAT THE OVEN TO 350°F. LINE A BAKING TRAY WITH parchment paper.

In a small saucepan, bring the water to a boil. Add the dried apricots, remove from the heat, and allow to soften for 15 minutes. Drain completely, pushing out all the water, and finely chop the apricots.

In a medium bowl, whisk together the flour, cornmeal, baking soda, and salt. In the bowl of a stand mixer fitted with a paddle attachment, combine the sugar and orange zest. With your fingers, gently rub the sugar and zest together until the mixture becomes sandy and fragrant. Add the butter to the bowl of a stand mixer and beat on medium speed until pale and fluffy, about 3 minutes. Add the rosemary and vanilla and beat. Add the eggs, one at a time, beating well after each addition. With the mixer on low, add the flour mixture and beat until just combined. Add the chopped apricots and beat until combined. Drop 2-tablespoon scoops of dough onto the prepared baking tray, spaced 1 inch apart. Bake for 10 to 12 minutes, turning the pan halfway through baking, until lightly browned on the edges. Repeat with the remaining dough. Transfer to a cooling rack and let cool.

MAKE AHEAD: The cookie dough can be made up to 3 days ahead and stored in the refrigerator or spooned onto 2 parchment-lined trays, frozen, then transferred to an airtight container or sealed plastic bag in the freezer for up to 1 month. Bake directly from the freezer, adding 1 to 2 minutes additional bake time.

STORE: Store the cookies in an airtight container for up to 4 days.

Smoky Peanut Brittle

Almost everyone loves old-fashioned peanut brittle. And almost everyone loves sweet and savory cocktail nuts. So why not combine the flavors of the two? This sweet and nutty peanut brittle has smoke and heat from pimentón de la Vera, a smoked paprika from La Vera, Spain, plus a drizzle of dark chocolate. The unique combination will keep people guessing and make their mouths water for more.

ACTIVE TIME: 25 minutes
TOTAL TIME: 50 minutes

Makes 1¼ pounds of brittle

PREHEAT THE OVEN TO 325°F. GREASE A 9 × 13-INCH PAN or line it with a nonstick baking mat.

Place the peanuts on a separate, ungreased and unlined baking tray and toast in the oven for 10 to 12 minutes, until light brown and fragrant.

In a medium saucepan, combine the granulated sugar, light brown sugar, and corn syrup. Cook over medium heat, stirring frequently. Monitor the temperature with a candy thermometer. In a small bowl, whisk together the pimentón de la Vera, cinnamon, cayenne, salt, and baking soda. When the cooking sugars reach 265°F, add the toasted peanuts to the pan. Continue to cook, stirring continuously, until the mixture reaches 305°F. Reduce the heat to low and add the butter and vanilla, stirring vigorously until incorporated. Turn off the heat and add the spice mixture. Stir continuously, until the mixture bubbles up. The mixture will be very foamy.

Pour the mixture onto the prepared pan. Working quickly with a greased offset spatula, gently spread the mixture to the edges of the pan. Use a light touch to keep the brittle foamy, which creates a delicate, crunchy texture. Allow the peanut brittle to cool and harden, about 15 minutes.

Meanwhile, melt the chocolate in a double boiler over low heat. When the brittle has cooled, use a spoon to drizzle chocolate evenly over the brittle. Place the brittle in the freezer until the chocolate has hardened, about 5 minutes. Break the brittle into pieces with your hands or a small mallet.

STORE: Layer pieces of peanut brittle with sheets of parchment paper in an airtight container and store at room temperature for up to 1 week.

1¼ cups roasted, unsalted peanuts

½ cup granulated sugar

½ cup firmly packed light brown sugar

½ cup light corn syrup

Heaping ½ teaspoon pimentón de la Vera (any smoked paprika is a fine substitute)

¼ teaspoon ground Vietnamese cinnamon

Heaping ¼ teaspoon ground cayenne

¼ teaspoon kosher salt

1 teaspoon baking soda

4 tablespoons (2 ounces) unsalted butter

1 teaspoon vanilla extract

3 ounces bittersweet chocolate, roughly chopped

SPECIAL EQUIPMENT

Deep-fry/candy thermometer

SAVORY, EARTHY, AND NUTTY

Winter Citrus Galette

ACTIVE TIME: 1 hour
TOTAL TIME: 3 hours

Serves 8

GALETTE DOUGH

1½ cups all-purpose flour

¾ teaspoon granulated sugar

¼ teaspoon kosher salt

9 tablespoons (4½ ounces)
cold unsalted butter,
cut into ½-inch cubes, divided

3 to 5 tablespoons ice water

CUMIN CARAMEL

½ cup granulated sugar

1 tablespoon light corn syrup

3 tablespoons water

¾ teaspoon ground cumin

2 tablespoons (1 ounce)
unsalted butter

¼ cup heavy cream

¼ teaspoon kosher salt

1 teaspoon finely grated
blood orange zest,
or the zest of any orange

(Continued)

One of chef Jean-Georges Vongerichten's most famous dishes is his roasted carrots with orange juice and cumin. It's one of my favorite vegetable dishes ever. Just thinking of it makes my mouth water—and made me wonder if the same pairing of orange and cumin that is so sublime in a savory dish could work just as beautifully in a sweet one. The answer is yes. This is one of my favorite recipes in the book: slightly bitter caramel, flaky, melt-in-your-mouth pastry, bright oranges, and just the slightest touch of smoky, earthy cumin. It might sound odd, but wait until you try it. It's sweet alchemy.

Galette Dough

IN A MEDIUM BOWL, COMBINE THE FLOUR, SUGAR, AND salt. With a pastry cutter or your hands, cut 3 tablespoons of the butter into the flour mixture until it resembles a coarse meal. Add the remaining 6 tablespoons of butter and cut it into the mixture until it forms pea-sized chunks. Drizzle 3 tablespoons of ice water into the mixture and toss with your hands just until the dough holds together. If there are some dry patches in the dough, drizzle on additional water and toss until a dough forms. Press the dough into an oval approximately 6 inches by 4 inches. Wrap it tightly in plastic wrap and let it rest for at least 1 hour in the fridge.

Cumin Caramel

IN A LARGE SAUCEPAN, COMBINE THE SUGAR, CORN syrup, and water. Brush down the sides of the pan with a pastry brush to be sure there's no sugar left there. Cook over medium heat until the mixture caramelizes and is a light amber color, 6 to 8 minutes. Remove from the heat and whisk in the cumin. Add the butter, cream, salt, and orange zest and stir to combine. Allow to cool and thicken.

(Continued)

ASSEMBLING THE GALETTE

2¼ pounds assorted winter citrus such as navel, cara cara, and blood oranges

¾ teaspoon cornstarch

1 large egg

2 teaspoons water

Pinch of kosher salt

1 tablespoon turbinado sugar (optional)

1½ teaspoons unsalted butter, melted

LIGHTLY FLOUR YOUR WORK SURFACE. LINE A BAKING tray with a nonstick baking mat or parchment paper. With a rolling pin, roll out the galette dough into a 12-inch round. Transfer the dough onto the prepared baking tray and place in the refrigerator. Chill the dough while you prepare the oranges.

Trim ½ inch off the top and bottom of each orange. Working carefully over a small bowl, cut the skin from its flesh, top to bottom, being sure to follow the curves down. Once the peel is removed, begin segmenting the orange by cutting away the flesh from the membrane on both sides. The orange segments should easily come out. Repeat this with the remaining segments. Place all the orange pieces into a fine-mesh sieve over a bowl and push down on them lightly to strain out excess moisture. Allow to stand for 10 minutes. Pat the oranges dry with a paper towel and separate the segments and slices. Toss the orange segments with the cornstarch and then stir them into the cooled cumin caramel.

Spoon the caramel-orange mixture onto the center of the chilled galette dough, leaving a 2½-inch border of dough. Fold the border in to partially cover the oranges, leaving a 5-inch opening in the middle. In a small bowl, prepare an egg wash by whisking the egg with the water and salt. Brush this egg wash onto the folded-over dough. Sprinkle the dough with the turbinado sugar, if using. Layer the orange slices over the opening of the galette, overlapping them slightly. The oranges should extend about ½ inch beyond the opening; they will shrink during baking. Brush the orange slices with the melted butter.

Chill the galette in the freezer until the dough is firm, 15 to 20 minutes. Preheat the oven to 375°F. Bake the chilled tart for about 1 hour, turning the pan halfway through baking, until its juices are bubbling and the crust is a deep golden brown. Let cool. Serve at room temperature.

STORE: The baked galette can be refrigerated overnight and reheated.

When I lived in L.A., we had a lime tree in our backyard that produced lots and lots of limes. Even after we shared them with the neighbors, there were a lot left for cooking and baking. This recipe is a great way to use them—you'll need 4 or 5. The cake is buttery and rich and studded with poppy seeds, and the lime cuts through the richness with a zing. The uncooked lime glaze creates a uniquely crunchy crust packed with lime zest and juice. This cake is an explosion of citrus in your mouth.

Lime Crunch Cake

ACTIVE TIME: 30 minutes
TOTAL TIME: 1 hour, 30 minutes

Serves 10

1 ⅓ cups all-purpose flour

1 teaspoon baking powder

Heaping ¼ teaspoon kosher salt

2 tablespoons poppy seeds

12 tablespoons (6 ounces) unsalted butter, at room temperature

1 cup firmly packed light brown sugar

3 large eggs, at room temperature

1 tablespoon plus 1 teaspoon finely grated lime zest, divided

¼ cup plus 3 tablespoons freshly squeezed lime juice, divided

½ cup confectioners' sugar, sifted

½ cup plus 2 teaspoons granulated sugar, divided

PREHEAT THE OVEN TO 350°F. GREASE AN 8-INCH ROUND pan and line the bottom with a circle of parchment paper.

Sift the flour, baking powder, and salt together into a medium bowl. Add the poppy seeds and whisk to combine. In the bowl of a standing mixer fitted with a paddle attachment, cream the butter and brown sugar on medium speed until light and fluffy, 3 to 4 minutes. Add the eggs and continue to beat until smooth. Add 1 tablespoon of the lime zest and 2 tablespoons of the lime juice and beat until incorporated. The batter will look curdled, but don't worry. Add the flour mixture and beat on low speed until just combined. Pour the batter into the prepared pan and smooth the top with an offset spatula. Bake for 40 to 42 minutes, until a wooden toothpick inserted into the center comes out clean.

Meanwhile, make a lime syrup by whisking together the remaining ¼ cup plus 1 tablespoon of lime juice, the remaining 1 teaspoon of lime zest, the confectioners' sugar, and ½ cup of the granulated sugar in a medium bowl. Whisk until the sugars dissolve.

While the cake is still warm and in the pan, poke it all over with a skewer and spoon the lime syrup over the top. You can lift and swirl the pan to help distribute the syrup. Allow the cake to rest for 30 minutes after adding the syrup, then turn it out of the pan. Dust the remaining 2 teaspoons of granulated sugar evenly over the glazed cake.

STORE: Cover and store at room temperature for up to 3 days.

SAVORY, EARTHY, AND NUTTY

Chewy Chocolate Devils

ACTIVE TIME: 15 minutes
TOTAL TIME: 1 hour

Makes 10 to 12 large cookies

2½ cups confectioners' sugar

½ cup Dutch-process cocoa powder

½ teaspoon ground Vietnamese cinnamon

2 teaspoons espresso powder

¾ teaspoon kosher salt

1 tablespoon urfa biber flakes

Whites from 3 large eggs, at room temperature

1 teaspoon vanilla extract

3 ounces bittersweet chocolate, roughly chopped

Rich, fudgy, and gooey with a little tingle of chile on the tip of your tongue—this is the best brownie cookie you've ever had. Be sure to use a good Dutch-process cocoa powder. Spending a little more on good-quality cocoa makes a big difference in the final result. But it's the urfa biber chile that really makes these cookies memorable. It's smoky and sultry, with a deceptive heat. A perfect pairing for dark chocolate.

PREHEAT THE OVEN TO 350°F. LINE TWO BAKING TRAYS with nonstick baking mats or lightly greased parchment paper.

In a large bowl, sift together the confectioners' sugar, cocoa powder, cinnamon, espresso powder, and salt. Add the urfa biber and whisk to combine. Add the egg whites and whisk until the batter is incorporated. Switch to a rubber spatula and stir in the vanilla and chopped chocolate. Chill the dough in the refrigerator for at least 30 minutes. Form 2-tablespoon mounds of batter and drop onto the prepared baking trays about 1 inch apart; the cookies will spread a bit. Bake for about 8 minutes, until the cookies begin cracking on the surface, then rotate the pans and bake for an additional 2 minutes, or until the edges are set. The centers should still be a little soft and gooey. Allow to cool for 10 minutes on the tray before transferring to cooling racks. To easily remove the cookies from the trays, lightly grease your spatula.

STORE: You can store these cookies in an airtight container at room temperature for up to 3 days.

OH, HOW I WANTED TO DRINK CHAI WHEN I WAS GROWING UP. WATCHING my elders begin their morning with a ritualistic cup of tea, I was eager to join the ranks of the tea drinkers. Every profound conversation in a Pakistani home must begin and end with a steaming hot cup of sweet, aromatic, spiced milk tea, so upon entering any Pakistani home, you'll hear, *Aap chai piyaange?* "Would you like to drink tea? Take a sip." Each family uses its own mix of spices, and blended together, these spices create complex and mysterious flavors that are even more enticing than the individual components.

Complex

AND

Mysterious

Cocoa Chai Granola

ACTIVE TIME: 15 minutes
TOTAL TIME: 1 hour, 20 minutes

Makes 1½ pounds

1½ cups thick rolled oats

½ cup quinoa, rinsed thoroughly

¼ cup unsweetened coconut chips
or flakes

¼ cup sunflower seeds

½ cup pistachio nuts

¼ cup plus 2 tablespoons mild olive oil
or coconut oil

¼ cup plus 2 tablespoons mild honey

½ cup granulated sugar

⅓ cup Dutch-process cocoa

½ teaspoon vanilla extract

1 teaspoon fennel seeds

1 teaspoon ground ginger

½ teaspoon ground cardamom

½ teaspoon ground Vietnamese
cinnamon

½ teaspoon freshly ground
black pepper

½ teaspoon kosher salt

½ teaspoon fleur de sel

This granola is a real game changer. It's loaded with grains, seeds, and nuts for the balance of crunchiness, and it has rich cocoa to satisfy those frequent chocolate cravings. The spices are a tasty surprise. They work together to create the unique flavor of chai. My favorite way to eat this is with cold almond milk and bananas. As with your favorite childhood cereal, the last couple spoonfuls of milk are incredibly tasty, full of chocolate and spice. Packaged with a bow, this granola also makes a beautiful hostess gift.

PREHEAT THE OVEN TO 275°F. GREASE A BAKING TRAY with mild olive oil.

In a large bowl, stir together the oats, quinoa, coconut, sunflower seeds, and pistachios. In a medium saucepan, whisk together the olive oil, honey, sugar, cocoa, and vanilla. Use a mortar and pestle to lightly crush the fennel seeds. Add the fennel, ginger, cardamom, cinnamon, black pepper, and salt to the olive oil mixture and whisk to combine. Cook over medium-high heat, whisking continuously, until the mixture is emulsified and begins to bubble around the edges. (The mixture will be thick and gloppy; it's supposed to be this way.) Pour the olive oil mixture over the oat mixture and stir until the dry ingredients are well coated.

Spread out the granola mixture on the prepared baking tray. Sprinkle with fleur de sel. Bake for 50 minutes, turning the pan halfway through baking. Turn off the oven and let the granola sit in the warm oven for another 15 minutes. Remove the pan from the oven and let the granola cool completely in the pan. Break into large clumps.

STORE: Store in an airtight container at room temperature for up to 3 weeks.

My amma made baklava on special occasions when I was growing up. It was floral and sticky with honey and loaded with nuts, which we all loved. But this baklava was inspired by a very different source: a good friend who frequently visits Turkey and once brought me baklava from Karaköy Güllüoglu, one of the country's most famous bakeries. It was divine, and I had to learn more about Turkish baklava. One I read about was made with pureed oranges. I was determined to create one like that, even though I've never tasted the original. It took eight tries to get the recipe just right: crispy, with a delicate spiced honey syrup, bitter and creamy orange, and an unexpected addition— sweet fennel pollen. It tastes like nothing you've ever had. There are so many beautiful flavors—and it's even better served with a dollop of unsweetened clotted cream.

Pastry Layers

REMOVE STEMS FROM THE ORANGES AND DISCARD. PLACE the whole oranges in a large saucepan and fill with enough water to cover the oranges. Weigh down the fruits with a heatproof plate or upside-down pot cover to keep them submerged. Bring to a boil over high heat, then reduce the heat to medium and simmer until the oranges are fork tender, about 25 minutes. Drain and let cool. Cut the oranges in half and remove any seeds. Transfer orange halves to the bowl of a food processor and puree until very smooth.

Place a fine-mesh sieve over a small bowl and line with a double layer of cheesecloth. Pour half the orange puree into the sieve. Gather the edges of the cheesecloth together to make a satchel and squeeze out as much liquid as possible, being sure to keep the syrup. Dump all the pulp into a medium bowl. Repeat with the remaining puree, transferring the pulp into the bowl with the rest. Reserve a total of ¼ cup of the liquid for the syrup and set aside the rest for another use (such as mixing into maple syrup for pancakes or French toast). When you are finished, you should have about 1¾ cups (or a little less) of pulp with the texture of mashed potatoes. To the bowl of pulp, add the orange marmalade, vanilla, and the salt.

(Continued)

Crispy Mandarin Baklava

ACTIVE TIME: 1 hour
TOTAL TIME: 2 hours

Makes 16 squares

PASTRY LAYERS

2 pounds mandarin oranges or other thin-skinned citrus (avoid clementines, which result in a bitter filling)

¼ cup orange marmalade

2 teaspoons vanilla extract

⅛ teaspoon kosher salt

1 cup whole hazelnuts

1 package 14 × 18-inch phyllo sheets, defrosted in the refrigerator

8 tablespoons (4 ounces) unsalted butter, melted

2 teaspoons fennel pollen

SYRUP

¼ cup mandarin orange liquid (reserved from pastry layers recipe)

¼ teaspoon kosher salt

1¼ cups water

¼ cup plus 2 tablespoons mild honey

1 cup granulated sugar

Two 4½-inch cinnamon sticks

⅜ teaspoon ground cloves

Preheat the oven to 300°F. Toast the hazelnuts on a baking tray for 12 minutes. While the nuts are still warm, place them on a clean kitchen towel. Rub the nuts with the towel until most of the dark outer skins have been removed. Separate the nuts from skins and transfer the nuts to the bowl of a food processor. Pulse until the nuts are chopped very small but not ground as fine as a nut flour. Increase the oven temperature to 350°F. Grease a 9 × 13-inch pan.

Unroll the phyllo dough and cover the sheets of dough with a piece of plastic wrap followed by a barely damp kitchen towel to prevent the dough from drying out. (Don't let the damp towel touch the dough.) Working quickly, lift the plastic wrap and towel to remove 1 sheet of phyllo dough and lay it in the pan. Carefully re-cover the remaining dough. Brush the top of the sheet with melted butter. To create the baklava, you will layer phyllo sheets, each brushed on top with butter, with the other ingredients distributed evenly across the phyllo sheet.

From the bottom, layer as follows:

3 buttered phyllo sheets, ¼ cup nuts
2 buttered phyllo sheets, ¼ cup nuts
2 buttered phyllo sheets, ¼ cup nuts
2 buttered phyllo sheets, ¼ cup nuts
3 buttered phyllo sheets, orange puree
1 buttered phyllo sheet, ½ teaspoon fennel pollen
1 buttered phyllo sheet, ½ teaspoon fennel pollen
1 buttered phyllo sheet, ½ teaspoon fennel pollen
12 buttered phyllo sheets and, finally, ½ teaspoon
    fennel pollen

With a sharp knife (I prefer serrated), cut the baklava pastry into 16 even rectangles. Run the knife around the edge of the pan to loosen the dough and prevent it from sticking to the sides during baking. This will help the layers to stay separate.

Bake at 350°F for 15 minutes. Lower the temperature to 300°F, turn the pan, and continue to bake for another 25 minutes. The phyllo will be puffy and golden brown. Let it cool completely.

Syrup

WHILE THE BAKLAVA PASTRY IS BAKING, PREPARE THE syrup. In a small saucepan, combine the reserved ¼ cup orange liquid (pressed from the pureed oranges) and the salt, water, honey, sugar, cinnamon sticks, and cloves. Bring the mixture to a boil over medium heat and stir. Let the mixture boil until it reduces to 1⅓ cups, 10 to 12 minutes. Remove the cinnamon sticks.

To put it together

MAKE SURE THE BAKLAVA PASTRY IS NOT STILL WARM when adding the syrup. Bring the syrup back up to a boil. With a large spoon, ladle the hot syrup evenly over the cooled baklava, being sure to get all the corners. Let it stand until the syrup is absorbed, about 45 minutes.

STORE: The baklava can be stored for up to 3 days at room temperature.

COMPLEX AND MYSTERIOUS

This pull-apart bread is easy to put together and looks so impressive with its swirls of dark, heavily spiced gingerbread cream and soft pears. In my house, we love the flavors of gingerbread—especially that little tickle of heat that comes from fresh ginger sparked with black peppercorns—so this bread disappears fast. But if you have any left over, it makes an amazing French toast a day or two later.

Gingerbread Cream and Pear Ribbon Bread

ACTIVE TIME: 55 minutes
TOTAL TIME: 3 hours, 20 minutes

Serves 10

Sweet Bread Dough

IN A SMALL SAUCEPAN OVER MEDIUM-LOW HEAT, combine the milk and the water. Heat until lukewarm. Whisk in the yeast and 1 teaspoon of the sugar. Set aside until frothy, about 3 minutes.

In the bowl of a stand mixer fitted with a dough hook, beat together the remaining ⅓ cup of sugar and the flour and salt. Add the eggs, vanilla, and yeast mixture and beat on low speed until a rough dough forms. Increase the speed to medium and beat until the dough comes together, 4 to 5 minutes. Add the butter 1 tablespoon at a time, beating after each addition to fully incorporate. Once all the butter is incorporated, continue to beat the dough until it is very smooth and elastic, another 4 to 5 minutes. Add the candied orange zest and beat on low speed for 1 minute.

Transfer the dough to a lightly oiled bowl and cover with plastic wrap. Let it rise until doubled in size, about 1 hour. Once the dough has doubled in size, punch it down to remove the air and chill in the refrigerator until ready to use.

Gingerbread Cream

IN A SMALL SAUCEPAN OVER MEDIUM-HIGH HEAT, combine the milk, ginger, cinnamon sticks, peppercorns, cardamom, nutmeg, and cloves. Bring to a boil, then remove the pan from the heat, cover, and let steep for 25 minutes. Strain the spiced milk through a fine-mesh sieve over a medium bowl and discard the solids. Return the spiced milk to the saucepan. Add the granulated sugar and bring the mixture to a simmer over medium heat.

(Continued)

SWEET BREAD DOUGH

⅓ cup whole milk

¼ cup water

2¼ teaspoons (1 package) active dry yeast

⅓ cup plus 1 teaspoon granulated sugar, divided

3 cups all-purpose flour

1 teaspoon kosher salt

2 large eggs

1 teaspoon vanilla extract

6 tablespoons (3 ounces) unsalted butter, at room temperature

3 tablespoons Candied Orange Zest, cut into ¼-inch pieces (page 26), or substitute store-bought candied orange (page 252) or 1 teaspoon finely grated orange zest

(Continued)

GINGERBREAD CREAM

2½ cups whole milk

1 tablespoon grated fresh ginger

Two 3½-inch cinnamon sticks

1 teaspoon cracked black peppercorns

3 crushed cardamom pods

¼ nutmeg seed

3 whole cloves

3 tablespoons granulated sugar

Yolks from 4 large eggs

¼ cup firmly packed dark muscovado sugar or dark brown sugar

3 tablespoons cornstarch

1 tablespoon unsulphured molasses

¼ teaspoon kosher salt

GLAZE

1 tablespoon whole milk

1 teaspoon freshly squeezed lemon juice

1 cup confectioners' sugar

Pinch of kosher salt

ASSEMBLING THE BREAD

1 firm Bosc pear with skin

1 large egg

2 teaspoons water

Pinch of kosher salt

2 tablespoons granulated sugar

In a medium bowl, whisk together the egg yolks, muscovado sugar, and cornstarch. When the milk mixture simmers, slowly pour about half of it into the egg mixture, at little at a time, whisking to combine after each addition. Pour the warm egg mixture back into the saucepan with the remaining milk mixture. Cook over medium heat, whisking continuously, until the mixture begins to bubble and thickens into a smooth custard. Continue cooking for 1 more minute.

Remove the custard from the heat and strain through a fine-mesh sieve over a medium bowl. Stir in the molasses and salt. Cover with plastic wrap, pressing it directly onto the surface of the custard to prevent a skin from forming.

Glaze

IN A SMALL BOWL, WHISK TOGETHER ALL THE INGREDI-ents until smooth.

Assembling the Bread

GREASE A 9 × 5-INCH LOAF PAN. CUT THE PEAR IN HALF lengthwise. Remove the core with a melon baller and cut out the stem with a paring knife. With a mandoline or knife, cut the pear halves into ⅛-inch slices. In a small bowl, whisk together the egg, water, and salt to make an egg wash.

Dust your work surface and rolling pin with a little flour. Place the chilled sweet bread dough on your work surface and use your hands to shape it into a rectangle. Using the rolling pin, roll the dough into a 12-inch by 20-inch rectangle. Spread the gingerbread cream on the left or right half of the dough only, leaving a ¼-inch border. Arrange the pear slices in a single layer on top of the cream. Fold the other half of the dough over, sandwiching the cream and pears between two layers of dough. (If the dough is warm and soft, chill in the refrigerator for 15 minutes to make it easier to handle.)

Cut the dough lengthwise into 4 equal strips. Cut 2 of the strips crosswise into 6 equal rectangles. Cut the other 2 strips crosswise into 4 equal squares. You will have 20 pieces of dough. Line up the pieces in the prepared loaf pan, cut edges up, alternating between small and large pieces randomly for visual effect. Don't be afraid to squish the pieces to fit them all in. Cover the pan loosely with plastic

wrap and allow the dough to rise until doubled in size, about 40 minutes.

Preheat the oven to 350°F. Brush the top of the dough with the egg wash. (You won't use it all.) Sprinkle the top with the sugar. Bake for 50 minutes, turning the pan after 30 minutes so it will bake evenly. If the top of the bread is browning too quickly, tent a piece of aluminum foil over it. Remove the pan from the oven and allow the bread to cool completely. Turn it out from the pan onto parchment and drizzle with the glaze.

STORE: This bread is best the day it's made, but it can be made 1 day ahead and stored in the refrigerator. Allow it to come to room temperature before serving.

COMPLEX AND MYSTERIOUS

Spiced Sweet Potato and Date Bread

This spice combination—clove, cinnamon, ginger, and nutmeg—is what fall tastes like. But this quick bread will surprise you with sweet potato and coconut oil instead of the traditional pumpkin and butter. They give the bread an unmatched moistness and just the slightest hint of tropical coconut flavor. The dates add a pleasant texture and flavor that will keep you baking loaves through the fall and into the winter.

ACTIVE TIME: 20 minutes
TOTAL TIME: 2 hours, 30 minutes

Makes 2 loaves

POSITION AN OVEN RACK IN THE CENTER OF THE OVEN. Preheat the oven to 350°F. Wrap the sweet potatoes tightly in aluminum foil and bake until tender, about 1 hour. Allow to cool, then remove the peel and discard. Mash the flesh finely. You will have about 1½ cups of mashed sweet potato.

Line the bottoms of two 8½ × 4½-inch loaf pans with parchment paper, cut to fit the pan with a 2-inch overhang on each side, and grease the sides and bottom generously with coconut oil.

In a large bowl, whisk together the granulated sugar, muscovado sugar, eggs and egg yolks, and the coconut oil. Add the mashed sweet potato, sour cream, and vanilla and whisk well to combine. In a medium bowl, sift together the flour, baking soda, salt, cloves, cinnamon, ginger, and nutmeg and whisk to combine. Using a rubber spatula, fold the flour mixture into the sweet potato mixture until just combined. Fold in the dates until evenly distributed. Divide the batter evenly between the prepared pans and sprinkle each loaf with 1 tablespoon of turbinado sugar.

Bake for 50 to 55 minutes, rotating the pans halfway through baking, until the loaves are golden brown and firm to the touch and a wooden toothpick inserted into the center comes out dry but with moist crumbs. Transfer to a cooling rack and let cool for 5 minutes, then turn the loaves out of the pan. Serve warm or at room temperature.

STORE: Wrapped tightly in plastic, the loaves will keep for 3 days at room temperature or for up to 1 month in the freezer.

2¼ pounds sweet potatoes, or 1½ cups pure canned pumpkin

1 cup coconut oil, melted and cooled to room temperature

1 cup granulated sugar

1 cup firmly packed light muscovado sugar or light brown sugar

2 large eggs plus the yolks from 2 large eggs, at room temperature

⅔ cup plus 2 tablespoons sour cream, at room temperature

2 teaspoons vanilla extract

2¼ cups all-purpose flour

2 teaspoons baking soda

1 teaspoon kosher salt

⅛ teaspoon ground cloves

1 teaspoon ground Vietnamese cinnamon

¼ teaspoon ground ginger

1 teaspoon freshly grated nutmeg

¾ cup medjool dates, firmly packed, pitted and roughly chopped

2 tablespoons turbinado sugar

Chocolate Blueberry Gelato Bonbons

ACTIVE TIME: 40 minutes
TOTAL TIME: Overnight

Makes 40 bonbons

1½ cups blueberries

⅓ to ½ cup granulated sugar (depending on how sweet the blueberries are)

1 teaspoon Chinese five spice powder

1½ teaspoons freshly squeezed lemon juice

½ cup heavy cream

1½ cups unsweetened coconut cream

12 ounces bittersweet chocolate, roughly chopped

3 tablespoons coconut oil

1 cup crushed chocolate wafer cookies

2 tablespoons sweetened shredded coconut

There are many different recipes for Chinese five spice powder. Most are made of some combination of star anise, cloves, cinnamon, Szechuan peppercorns, ginger, and fennel seeds. You can try different mixtures until you find your favorite, but all these spices add warmth and complexity to desserts, and they go especially well with the creamy coldness of gelato. Here I've combined the classic Chinese spice mix with the lush flavor of coconut and sweet blueberries. As the bonbon melts on your tongue, you get chocolate, coconut cream, blueberry, and a long, lingering spiced finish.

IN A SMALL SAUCEPAN, COMBINE THE BLUEBERRIES, sugar, and Chinese five spice powder. Bring to a boil over medium-high heat and then reduce the heat to low. Simmer until the blueberries soften, give up their juices, and begin to pop, 3 to 5 minutes. Remove from the heat, add the lemon juice, and allow to cool.

Puree the blueberry mixture in a food processor or with an immersion blender. Strain the puree through a coarse-mesh sieve over a medium bowl to remove most of the chewy skins. (It's okay to leave a few.) Stir in the heavy cream and coconut cream. Refrigerate until completely cold, for several hours or overnight. It's important that the mixture be thoroughly chilled.

Transfer the cold mixture to an ice cream maker and process according to the manufacturer's instructions. After processing, freeze the gelato for several hours to set.

Line a baking tray with parchment paper. Scoop the gelato onto the tray in tablespoon-sized balls. You will have about 40. Place the tray in the freezer.

(Continued)

STORE: The bonbons can be stored in the freezer in an airtight container for up to 1 week. To serve, remove them from the freezer, place on a plate or serving platter, and let stand for 10 minutes to soften the ice cream.

In a double boiler, melt the chocolate and coconut oil and whisk to combine. Remove from the heat and let cool to room temperature. Place the cookie crumbs in a small bowl. Insert a wooden skewer into a frozen scoop of gelato and dip the entire scoop in chocolate. Gently tap the skewer on the edge of the double boiler to remove excess chocolate. Press the bottom of the chocolate-covered bonbon in the cookie crumbs and place the bonbon, crumbs down, on the same parchment-lined baking tray. Twist the skewer to remove it, and press a pinch of shredded coconut over the hole where the skewer was. Return the pan of bonbons to the freezer, to rechill before serving.

This recipe was created on a lazy Sunday afternoon during a visit to my amma's house. She had a freezer full of homemade puff pastry scraps that I didn't want to waste, so I checked out the spices Amma had in her pantry and created my own *masala*, or spice mix. I like how this combination of flavors blooms on the tongue. The cinnamon comes first, followed by a gentle hit of clove. My amma had turbinado sugar in her pantry, too. Palmiers are traditionally made with granulated sugar, but I use turbinado for its caramel flavor and extra crunch. Because turbinado sugar melts more slowly than granulated sugar, you can be more generous with it without worrying about burning anything.

IN A SMALL BOWL, WHISK TOGETHER THE SUGAR, POPPY seeds, cinnamon, cloves, and ¼ teaspoon of the salt. Sprinkle 2 tablespoons of the sugar mixture evenly over your work surface. Unfold the puff pastry and place it on the sugar-dusted surface. Sprinkle another 2 tablespoons of the sugar mixture on top of the puff pastry. With a rolling pin, roll the dough into a rectangle 12 inches by 16 inches, flipping the dough as needed and sprinkling the dough with another 2 tablespoons of the sugar mixture each time you do. (The sugar will keep the dough from sticking; don't use any flour.) Use up all the sugar, making sure each side gets the same amount. When you are finished rolling out the dough, prick it all over with a fork.

In a small bowl, prepare an egg wash by whisking the egg with the water and a pinch of the salt.

To make the classic butterfly-like palmier shape, turn the dough so that the long sides of the rectangle are parallel with the edge of the countertop. Trim the edges of the dough to make a rectangle that is precisely 12 inches by 16 inches. Using a knife, make an indentation to mark the centerline of the rectangle, measuring exactly 8 inches from the short sides. Fold the right and left edges of the dough in 2 inches from the sides, and brush egg wash over the folded dough. Fold the dough in another 2 inches from both sides, and brush with egg wash. Repeat a third time. There should be

My Masala Palmiers

ACTIVE TIME: 30 minutes
TOTAL TIME: 1 hour, 30 minutes

 *Makes* 4 dozen palmiers

½ cup turbinado sugar

1½ teaspoons poppy seeds

2½ teaspoons ground Vietnamese cinnamon

¾ teaspoon ground cloves

¼ teaspoon kosher salt, plus a pinch

¾ pound all-butter puff pastry, thawed if frozen

1 large egg

2 teaspoons water

MAKE AHEAD: You can store the rolled, unsliced dough in the refrigerator for 1 day or in the freezer for up to 1 month. Wrap the dough in wax paper and then aluminum foil instead of using plastic wrap. Plastic wrap can trap condensation. If frozen, thaw for a few hours in the refrigerator before slicing and baking.

STORE: Store in an airtight container for up to 3 days.

a narrow, ¼-inch space at the center of the rectangle when the turns are complete. Brush this space with egg wash. Run a rolling pin very gently over the dough from top to bottom, then fold the right side over the left and run a rolling pin over the dough again. Roll in parchment paper or plastic wrap and chill the dough in the freezer until firm, about 30 minutes.

Preheat the oven to 375°F. Line two baking trays with parchment paper or nonstick baking mats.

Cut the chilled dough crosswise into ¼-inch-thick slices. Place 2 inches apart on the prepared baking trays. You will need to bake these in batches. Bake for about 12 minutes, until the bottom is light brown. Flip the palmiers and cook for an additional 8 to 9 minutes, until the top is golden. The palmiers will crisp up as they cool.

Chocolate and spice and everything nice is the best way to describe this tantalizing bark I created for a local television segment. It's chocolate indulgence, loaded with nuts and dried sour cherries, laced with sweet, earthy, and smoky spices, and finished with a light sprinkling of fleur de sel. Best, this bar is easy and quick to make, which is good because I always eat at least a quarter of it as soon as it's done .

PREHEAT THE OVEN TO 350°F. ROAST THE CASHEWS AND almonds on a baking tray for 8 minutes. Add the pistachios and continue to roast all the nuts until lightly toasted, an additional 3 to 5 minutes. Allow to cool, then coarsely chop the nuts.

Remove stem and seeds from the chile and discard. Tear the chile into pieces. In a small skillet over medium heat, combine the chile, star anise, fennel seeds, cloves, and cinnamon stick. Warm the spices until they are fragrant and the chile softens, about 3 minutes. Transfer to a coffee grinder and grind until very fine. Measure out 2 teaspoons of the spice mixture and set the rest aside for another use. (It's great in hot chocolate or sprinkled on chicken before grilling.)

Melt the chocolate in a double boiler over gently simmering water. (Or melt in the microwave at 50 percent power in 45 second bursts, stirring between bursts, until fully melted.) Add the oil and espresso powder and the 2 teaspoons of ground spice mixture to the melted chocolate and whisk to incorporate. Stir in the chopped nuts and the cherries. Line a baking tray with a nonstick baking mat or parchment paper. Use an offset spatula to spread the chocolate mixture evenly over the baking tray. Sprinkle with the fleur de sel and refrigerate until firm, about 45 minutes. Once cool, break the bark into pieces and serve.

STORE: Store the bark tightly covered in the refrigerator for up to 1 week. The spices will deepen in flavor over time.

Bittersweet Chile and Cinnamon Bark

ACTIVE TIME: 30 minutes
TOTAL TIME: 1 hour, 30 minutes

Makes about 1¼ pounds

¾ cup unsalted, raw whole cashews

¼ cup unsalted, raw whole almonds, with skin

¼ cup unsalted, roasted, shelled pistachios

1 large ancho chile

1 star anise pod

¼ teaspoon fennel seeds

3 whole cloves

One 2½-inch cinnamon stick

10 ounces bittersweet chocolate, finely chopped

1 teaspoon coconut oil or any neutral flavored oil

½ teaspoon espresso powder

¾ cup dried sour cherries, roughly chopped

¼ teaspoon fleur de sel

Apple Cider Jellies

ACTIVE TIME: 35 minutes
TOTAL TIME: Overnight

 *Makes* 60 jellies

2¼ cups Mulled Cider
(page 120)

3 cups granulated sugar, divided

½ cup firmly packed
light brown sugar

¾ cup light corn syrup

¾ cup plus 2 tablespoons
(2 packages) liquid pectin

¼ teaspoon kosher salt

1 teaspoon citric acid

SPECIAL EQUIPMENT

Deep-fry/candy thermometer

My inspiration for these little jellies is the oh-so-French *pate de fruit*, or fruit paste. In France, you find these little jewels of concentrated flavor in high-end patisseries. When made correctly, they are the perfect balance of fruit—tart and sweet—with a smooth bite. (Want them a little more sour? Increase the citric acid by ¼ teaspoon.) Traditionally, *pate de fruit* is made with fruit puree, but this updated version has an all-American modern twist: spiced apple cider.

GREASE AN 8-INCH SQUARE PAN AND LINE WITH PARCHMENT paper, leaving 1-inch overhangs on two sides of the pan.

Combine the mulled cider, 2 cups of the granulated sugar, and the light brown sugar and corn syrup in a medium saucepan over medium-high heat. Cook, whisking continuously, until the sugars dissolve and the mixture comes to a boil. Pour the pectin into a medium bowl, then pour half the mulled cider mixture into the pectin, whisking continuously. Whisk until smooth. Pour the pectin mixture into the saucepan with the remaining cider mixture. Bring to a boil and cook until the mixture reaches 225°F on a candy thermometer. Remove the pan from the heat and whisk in the salt. Working quickly, strain the hot mixture through a fine-mesh sieve into the prepared square pan. Let it sit until completely cool, about 1 hour.

In a small bowl, whisk together the remaining 1 cup of granulated sugar and the citric acid. Sprinkle a thin layer of the sugar mixture over the jelly. Place a piece of parchment paper on top of the jelly and invert it onto a baking tray. Peel the original piece of parchment paper off the bottom of the jelly and sprinkle with a thin layer of sugar mixture. Cut the jelly into 1-inch squares, then toss each jelly candy in the remaining sugar mixture to coat. You can also have fun with the shapes and cut small rectangles, triangles, or circles.

STORE: Layer these jellies with sheets of parchment paper in an airtight container and store for up to 2 weeks at room temperature. Keep the excess sugar mixture in a separate container and toss the jellies in it again before serving.

Banana bread is an American staple. The smell is familiar and comfortable, whether your mom made banana bread at home, bought it at the grocery store, or picked up a loaf at the local bakery. But this recipe isn't your typical banana bread. It's made with barely ripe bananas baked with nutty buckwheat flour, rich coconut palm sugar, and spiced toffee. (Don't use mushy overripe bananas for this cake. Mushy bananas will make a mushy cake.) The finished cake has the texture of a chewy blondie, and the caramel toffee's warm and enticing spices pop in your mouth. It looks and tastes stunning served alone or with a dollop of mascarpone.

PREHEAT THE OVEN TO 350°F. GREASE AN 8-INCH SQUARE pan and line it with a piece of parchment paper long enough to create a 1-inch overhang.

With the flat side of a knife, press lightly on the cardamom pods until they crack but are not crushed. In a skillet over medium heat, toast the cracked cardamom pods and star anise until fragrant, about 2 minutes. Slice the vanilla bean lengthwise and scrape out the seeds. Put the vanilla bean seeds and ½ cup plus 1 tablespoon of the light brown sugar into a small bowl and rub between your fingers to combine.

In a medium saucepan, combine the toasted cardamom and star anise, the vanilla bean pod, the vanilla-scented light brown sugar, 9 tablespoons of the butter, the corn syrup, and the lemon juice. Bring to a boil over medium heat, stirring continuously. Once the mixture starts to boil, cook until the caramel is foamy and thick, no longer than 1 more minute. (I like to time this; if you boil it for longer than 1 minute, the caramel will harden when it bakes.) Pour the caramel (including the whole spices) into the prepared square pan. Peel the bananas and cut in half lengthwise. Lay the bananas cut-side down in the caramel.

(Continued)

Toffee Banana Upside-Down Cake

ACTIVE TIME: 25 minutes
TOTAL TIME: 1 hour, 10 minutes

Serves 12

6 cardamom pods

4 star anise pods

1 vanilla bean

1 cup plus 1 tablespoon firmly packed light brown sugar

17 tablespoons (2 sticks plus 1 tablespoon; 8½ ounces) unsalted butter, divided

1 tablespoon light corn syrup

½ teaspoon freshly squeezed lemon juice

2 large barely ripe bananas

1 cup coconut palm sugar

2 teaspoons vanilla extract

2 large eggs, at room temperature

1 cup all-purpose flour

½ cup buckwheat flour

1 teaspoon baking powder

⅛ teaspoon kosher salt

COMPLEX AND MYSTERIOUS

In the bowl of a stand mixer fitted with a paddle attachment, beat the remaining 8 tablespoons of butter, the coconut palm sugar, and the remaining ½ cup of light brown sugar until light and fluffy, about 3 minutes. Add the vanilla extract and beat to combine. Add the eggs, one at a time, beating well after each addition. Beat until fully incorporated. In a medium bowl, whisk together the all-purpose flour, buckwheat flour, baking powder, and salt. Add the flour mixture to the butter mixture and beat on low speed until no streaks of flour remain, stopping to scrape down the sides of the bowl as needed. Pour the batter over the bananas and spread it evenly.

Bake for 35 to 40 minutes, turning the pan halfway through baking, until a wooden toothpick inserted into the center of the cake comes out clean. Allow to cool, then invert onto a plate.

Za'atar is a blend of dried herbs, sesame seeds, and sumac that has been used for centuries. The particular choice of herbs and how the ingredients are proportioned varies from culture to culture and family to family. A family's za'atar recipe is often a closely guarded secret. I like my za'atar heavy with thyme and sesame and brightened with sumac. The woodsy and nutty flavors work perfectly in this recipe: the musty flavor of the figs gets a puckery freshness from the sumac, and the herbs give deep flavor to the pistachio sugar. This recipe makes a lot of bars, but you can freeze the dough and make a fresh batch anytime.

Fig Filling

IN A MEDIUM SAUCEPAN, BRING THE FIGS, RAISINS, WATER, lemon juice, and salt to a boil. Reduce the heat to low and simmer, covered, for 15 minutes. Remove the cover and simmer for an additional 15 minutes or so to reduce the liquid. The mixture is ready when the fruit is nice and plump and a rubber spatula run across the bottom of the pan leaves a clear trail. Stir in the lemon zest. Let cool, then transfer to the bowl of a food processor and puree until smooth. Tightly cover the bowl with plastic wrap and store in the refrigerator until needed.

Dough

IN THE BOWL OF A STAND MIXER FITTED WITH A PADDLE attachment, beat the butter, sugar, and lemon zest on medium until light and fluffy, 3 to 4 minutes. Scrape down the bowl with a rubber spatula. Add the egg white and vanilla and beat until incorporated. Scrape down the bowl again and add the all-purpose flour and whole wheat flour. Beat on low speed until combined. Divide the dough in half. On a lightly floured piece of parchment paper, flatten and shape 1 piece of dough into a 15-inch by 11-inch rectangle. Slide the parchment and dough onto a baking sheet. Lightly flour

(Continued)

Figgy Bars

ACTIVE TIME: 1 hour
TOTAL TIME: 1 hour, 20 minutes

Makes 5 dozen cookies

FIG FILLING

1¼ cups firmly packed dried black mission figs, stemmed and roughly chopped

¾ cup firmly packed dark raisins

2 cups water

2 teaspoons freshly squeezed lemon juice

¼ teaspoon kosher salt

2 teaspoons finely grated lemon zest

DOUGH

8 tablespoons (4 ounces) unsalted butter

½ cup granulated sugar

½ teaspoon finely grated lemon zest

White from 1 large egg (reserve the yolk for assembling the bars)

½ teaspoon vanilla extract

1 cup all-purpose flour

½ cup whole wheat flour

ASSEMBLING THE BARS

Yolk from 1 large egg (reserved from the dough recipe)

1 teaspoon water

⅛ teaspoon kosher salt, plus a pinch

Heaping 2 tablespoons finely chopped pistachio nuts

1½ teaspoons za'atar

¼ cup turbinado sugar

another piece of parchment paper and repeat with the other piece of dough. Transfer the two baking pans to the refrigerator and chill until the dough is firm, about 15 minutes. Trim the edges of each rectangle to create straight sides and then cut each rectangle of dough lengthwise into 5 equal strips, about 3 inches wide by 11 inches long. Wrap the pans tightly with plastic wrap and chill for at least 1 hour and as long as overnight.

Assembling the Bars

PREHEAT THE OVEN TO 350°F. LINE TWO BAKING TRAYS with nonstick baking mats or parchment paper.

In a small bowl, prepare an egg wash by whisking the egg yolk with the water and a pinch of the salt. Transfer the fig filling into a plastic piping bag or a small ziplock bag and snip off the corner of the bag. Remove the dough strips from the refrigerator and pipe a thick row of filling down the center of a strip of dough. Brush egg wash along both long edges of the strip and carefully fold one long edge of the dough up and over the filling, gently pressing to seal to the other long edge. Repeat with the remaining strips. Return the pan to the refrigerator and chill the filled strips until solid, at least 30 minutes and as long as overnight.

In a small bowl, combine the pistachios, za'atar, the remaining ⅛ teaspoon of salt, and the turbinado sugar. Brush the top of each chilled log with egg wash and sprinkle generously with the pistachio sugar. Cut each log diagonally into 7 equal pieces and place ½ inch apart on the prepared baking trays. Bake for 18 to 20 minutes, turning the pan halfway through baking, until golden brown. Repeat for a second batch to bake all 5 dozen cookies. Allow to cool completely in the pan.

When I was eleven, my favorite cookbook was Martha Stewart's *Entertaining*. I read it again and again—sometimes I just stared at the pictures—and I cooked every single dessert in that book. One of the first ones I tried was an oven-baked pear. It was simple, but like these maple cream pears, it was a showstopper. In this recipe, the pears give up their juices, which then reduce with the maple syrup, Chinese five spice powder, and cream to make a sauce so good you'll want to drink it. I still have the *Entertaining* book; its pages are stained and stuck together. When I appeared on *The Martha Stewart Show* a couple of years ago, I showed the well-loved book off to Martha herself.

PREHEAT THE OVEN TO 375°F. GENEROUSLY GREASE THE bottom and sides of a 9 × 13-inch pan with the butter.

Peel the pears and cut in half lengthwise. Use a melon baller to remove the cores and cut out the stems with a paring knife. Place the pears cut side down in the prepared pan. In a medium bowl, whisk together the cream, maple syrup, sugar, five spice powder, ginger, and salt. Pour the cream mixture over the pears, making sure to coat each pear. The liquid will come about halfway up the sides of the pears.

Bake for up to 50 minutes, until the pears are tender, using a spoon to baste the pears about every 15 minutes. If the pears are not tender after 50 minutes, cover the baking dish with aluminum foil to prevent the sauce from reducing further while the pears finish cooking. Serve the pears warm with the sauce spooned over the top.

STORE: This dessert can be stored in the refrigerator for up to 2 days. Allow it to come to room temperature and then warm in the oven at 350°F.

Smothered Maple Cream Pears

ACTIVE TIME: 25 minutes
TOTAL TIME: 1 hour, 5 minutes

Serves 8

2 tablespoons (1 ounce) unsalted butter, at room temperature

4 ripe d'Anjou pears

1½ cups heavy cream

¾ cup pure Grade B maple syrup

¼ cup plus 1 tablespoon granulated sugar

¾ teaspoon Chinese five spice powder

1 teaspoon ground ginger

¼ teaspoon kosher salt

Perfect Pumpkin Pancakes

ACTIVE TIME: 20 minutes
TOTAL TIME: 40 minutes

Serves 4

1 cup all-purpose flour

¼ cup whole wheat flour

2 tablespoons granulated sugar

1½ teaspoons baking powder

½ teaspoon baking soda

1 teaspoon ground Vietnamese cinnamon

¾ teaspoon ground ginger

¼ teaspoon ground cloves

¼ teaspoon freshly grated nutmeg

¼ teaspoon kosher salt

1¼ cups buttermilk, at room temperature, divided

2 large eggs, at room temperature, lightly beaten

4 tablespoons (2 ounces) unsalted butter, melted

2 teaspoons vanilla extract

¾ cup pure canned pumpkin

With the warm and comforting flavors of cinnamon, ginger, clove, and nutmeg, these pumpkin pancakes are the epitome of a cozy fall breakfast. They are a weekend favorite in my home. The trick to tender pancakes is to avoid overmixing the batter. It's okay to have small lumps in the batter, and overmixing will make the pancakes tough. Serve these hot from the griddle with butter and maple syrup.

PREHEAT THE OVEN TO 250°F.

In a large bowl, whisk together the all-purpose flour, whole wheat flour, sugar, baking powder, baking soda, cinnamon, ginger, cloves, nutmeg, and salt. In a medium bowl, whisk together 1 cup of the buttermilk and the eggs, butter, and vanilla. Add the buttermilk mixture to the flour mixture and whisk until barely combined. In another medium bowl, whisk together the pumpkin and the remaining ¼ cup of buttermilk. Using a rubber spatula, gently fold the pumpkin mixture into the batter.

Heat a skillet over medium-high heat. Lightly grease the skillet and cook the pancakes in batches. Spoon about ¼ cup batter onto the pan per pancake. Cook until golden brown on the bottom and slightly dry looking and bubbly on the top, 2 to 3 minutes. Use a metal spatula to flip each pancake and cook on the second side until cooked through, about 1 minute. Transfer the pancakes from the skillet to a baking tray, cover with aluminum foil, and keep warm in the oven while you cook more.

Pista barfi is one of my favorite South Asian desserts. It's made with condensed milk and sugar, cooked slowly until the dessert solidifies, and spiced with saffron and cardamom, a magical combination. Here I used that same delicious mixture of spices in a rich butter cake. A bite into this moist cake takes me back to holidays and family gatherings when it was served as a special treat.

Saffron Pistachio Tea Cake

ACTIVE TIME: 15 minutes
TOTAL TIME: 1 hour, 30 minutes

Serves 10

Tea Cake

PREHEAT THE OVEN TO 350°F. GREASE A 9 × 5-INCH LOAF pan and line the bottom with parchment paper.

In a coffee grinder or food processor, pulse the unsalted pistachio pieces with 1 tablespoon of the all-purpose flour to make a fine meal. Be careful not to overprocess the nuts or they will become oily.

In a medium bowl, whisk together the pistachio meal, almond flour, the remaining ¼ cup plus 3 tablespoons all-purpose flour, and the salt, baking powder, and cardamom. In a small bowl, combine the granulated sugar and lemon zest and rub the mixture between your fingers to release the lemon oils. In the bowl of a stand mixer fitted with a paddle attachment, beat the butter and lemon-sugar mixture on medium speed until light and fluffy, about 4 minutes. Add the eggs one at a time, beating well after each addition. Add the pistachio mixture all at once and beat on low speed to combine, pausing to scrape down the sides of the bowl as needed.

Spoon the batter into the prepared pan and smooth the top with an offset spatula or the back of a spoon. Bake for about 45 minutes, until a wooden toothpick inserted into the center of the cake comes out clean. Allow the cake to cool in the pan for 20 minutes, then run a knife around the sides, turn out the loaf, and transfer to a cooling rack, right side up.

(Continued)

TEA CAKE

¾ cup unsalted roasted pistachio pieces

½ cup all-purpose flour, divided

1⅓ cups natural almond flour (blanched is a fine substitute)

½ teaspoon kosher salt

¼ teaspoon baking powder

1½ teaspoons ground cardamom

1 cup granulated sugar

1 teaspoon finely grated lemon zest

14 tablespoons (7 ounces) unsalted butter, at room temperature

4 large eggs, at room temperature

SAFFRON GLAZE

2 tablespoons whole milk

⅛ teaspoon saffron threads

1¾ cups confectioners' sugar, sifted

1½ teaspoons freshly squeezed lemon juice

1 tablespoon finely chopped unsalted roasted pistachio nuts, for garnish

STORE: Store the cake in an airtight container at room temperature for up to 3 days.

Saffron Glaze

WHILE THE CAKE COOLS, MAKE THE GLAZE. COMBINE THE milk and saffron threads in a microwave-safe bowl and warm in the microwave for 30 seconds. Cover and allow to steep for 5 minutes. The milk will be tinted a rich yellow. In a medium bowl, whisk together the confectioners' sugar, lemon juice, and saffron-infused milk. To glaze the cake, place a plate under the cooling rack to catch any drips, then spoon the glaze over the cake, spreading it evenly so the glaze covers the top and flows down the sides. To garnish, sprinkle a row of chopped, roasted pistachios lengthwise down the center of the cake.

Decadent Chocolate Cardamom Torte

My niece is only nine, but she's a chocoholic. I think that's partly my influence. She loves to make a mess of sophisticated chocolate desserts like this one. It's an easy update of the flourless chocolate cake that was so popular a decade ago. The original is decadent, dense, and fudgy, but in my cake for Eden the richness of the chocolate is balanced by the acidic blackberries, bright cardamom, and floral rose water. Your dinner guests are guaranteed to love it as much as my little chocolate monster does.

ACTIVE TIME: 30 minutes
TOTAL TIME: 1 hour, 30 minutes

Serves 12

Chocolate Torte

PREHEAT THE OVEN TO 375°F. GREASE A 9-INCH ROUND springform pan. Line the bottom of the pan with a circle of parchment paper, and line the sides of the pan with a long strip of parchment paper. Place the pan on a baking tray.

In a double boiler, melt the chocolate and butter. Once melted, whisk until smooth. Add the sugar and whisk until dissolved. Transfer the mixture to the bowl of a stand mixer fitted with the paddle attachment. Add the eggs and vanilla and beat on low speed until the batter is glossy. Add the flour and salt and beat until combined.

Pour the batter into the prepared pan and bake for 20 minutes. The edges of the cake will puff up and the center will be loose and sunken. Let cool, then refrigerate while you prepare the glaze.

CHOCOLATE TORTE

7 ounces bittersweet chocolate, roughly chopped

14 tablespoons (7 ounces) unsalted butter, cut into ½-inch cubes

¾ cup granulated sugar

5 large eggs, at room temperature, lightly beaten

1 teaspoon vanilla extract

1 tablespoon all-purpose flour

½ teaspoon kosher salt

Blackberry Compote

IN A MEDIUM SAUCEPAN OVER MEDIUM-LOW HEAT, COMbine half the blackberries with the sugar and bring to a simmer. Cook until the sugar dissolves and the berries release their juices, about 2 minutes. Remove the pan from the heat and add the salt, lemon juice, and rose water. Allow to cool, then add the remaining blackberries.

BLACKBERRY COMPOTE

¾ pound fresh blackberries

2 to 3 tablespoons granulated sugar, to taste

Pinch of kosher salt

½ teaspoon freshly squeezed lemon juice

½ teaspoon rose water

(Continued)

(Continued)

COMPLEX AND MYSTERIOUS

3 cardamom pods

One 3-inch cinnamon stick

½ cup heavy cream

2 ounces bittersweet chocolate,
finely chopped

½ teaspoon light corn syrup

Whipped cream, for garnish
(recipe on page 88)

Cardamom Glaze

CRUSH THE CARDAMOM PODS TO REVEAL THE DARK
seeds inside. (The flat side of a chef's knife against a cutting board works well for this.) In a small saucepan over medium-high heat, combine the crushed cardamom pods, cinnamon stick, and cream. Bring to a boil, then remove the pan from the heat, cover, and let steep for 30 minutes. Strain the spiced cream through a fine-mesh sieve over a medium bowl and discard the solids. Return the spiced cream to the saucepan and bring to a boil over medium-high heat.

In a small bowl, combine the chocolate and corn syrup. When the spiced cream boils, pour it over the chocolate. Let it stand for 1 minute to melt the chocolate, then whisk until smooth. Use immediately.

To put it all together

SET A COOLING RACK OVER A BAKING TRAY. REMOVE
the chilled chocolate torte from the springform pan. (It can help to run a small knife around the bottom of the pan to loosen the edges.) Invert the torte onto a plate, peel away the parchment paper, and place the torte right side up on a serving platter.

Spoon the cardamom glaze over the torte, spreading it evenly so the glaze covers the top and flows down the sides. Return the torte to the refrigerator to chill until the glaze sets, about 20 minutes. Remove it from the refrigerator and allow it to come to room temperature. Serve with blackberry compote and whipped cream.

STORE: The torte can be stored in the refrigerator for up to 3 days.

As the name suggests, this crumble started as a classic linzer torte. The key to a great linzer torte is the right balance of filling and spiced, lightly sweetened dough. This linzer crumble, which shows off luscious late-summer fruits such as plums and nectarines, has the added crunch of hazelnuts and the mellow earthiness of coriander mixed into the comfortable and familiar blend of nutmeg, clove, and cinnamon. I like my fruit on the tart side, but you can add more sugar to the filling if you wish. Be sure to taste your fruit filling first and adjust the sugar accordingly.

PREHEAT THE OVEN TO 300°F. TOAST THE HAZELNUTS ON a baking tray for 12 minutes. While the nuts are still warm, place them on a clean kitchen towel. Rub the nuts with the towel until most of the dark outer skins have been removed. Allow the hazelnuts to cool, then roughly chop.

In a skillet over medium heat, toast the coriander, shaking the pan, until light golden and fragrant, 1 to 2 minutes. Use a mortar and pestle to coarsely grind the toasted coriander.

Increase the oven temperature to 375°F. Line a baking tray with parchment paper and place a 10-inch round pan on the tray, to catch any drips during baking.

In a medium bowl, stir together the chopped hazelnuts, toasted coriander, ¼ cup of the granulated sugar, and the muscovado sugar, flour, cinnamon, nutmeg, cloves, and ¼ teaspoon of the salt. Add the melted butter and orange zest and toss to combine. Press the mixture into clumps with your fingers to make the linzer crumble topping.

In a large bowl, toss together the nectarines, plums, and lemon juice. In a small bowl, whisk together the remaining ¾ to 1 cup of granulated sugar (depending on the sweetness of the fruit), the tapioca flour, and the remaining ⅛ teaspoon of salt. Add to the fruit mixture and toss gently to coat.

(Continued)

Summer Stone Fruit and Linzer Crumble

ACTIVE TIME: 30 minutes
TOTAL TIME: 1 hour, 15 minutes

Serves 10 to 12

⅓ cup plus 1 tablespoon hazelnuts with skins

¾ teaspoon whole coriander seeds

1 to 1¼ cups granulated sugar, divided

¼ cup firmly packed dark muscovado sugar or dark brown sugar

1¼ cups all-purpose flour

2 teaspoons ground Vietnamese cinnamon

Scant ¼ teaspoon freshly grated nutmeg

¼ teaspoon ground cloves

¼ teaspoon plus ⅛ teaspoon kosher salt, divided

8 tablespoons (4 ounces) unsalted butter, melted

1 teaspoon freshly grated orange zest

2 pounds ripe nectarines, pitted and cut into ½-inch wedges

(Continued)

COMPLEX AND MYSTERIOUS

1 pound ripe plums, pitted and cut into ½-inch wedges (black, red, or a combination of any seasonal plums)

1 tablespoon freshly squeezed lemon juice

3½ tablespoons tapioca flour

1 cup raspberries

Transfer half the fruit mixture into the round pan and top with ½ cup of the raspberries. Add the remaining fruit mixture, then add the remaining raspberries. Top evenly with the crumble topping.

Bake for 30 minutes, then reduce the oven temperature to 350°F and bake an additional 15 minutes or so, until bubbly and golden. Serve warm or at room temperature. This is great with ice cream or whipped cream (recipe on page 88) or just on its own.

MAKE AHEAD: The linzer crumble topping can be stored in the refrigerator for up to 3 days or in the freezer for up to 1 month. Bake directly from the freezer, adding 5 to 10 minutes to the baking time.

Glossary

ALLSPICE TO ZA'ATAR

ALLSPICE

Allspice got its name from its flavor and aroma, a mélange of warm spices like nutmeg, cinnamon, and clove. The fruit of a Caribbean tree, allspice berries are picked when green and dried before use. The dry, reddish-brown berries are popular around the world, often used in European, African, and Middle Eastern dishes and in many traditional foods of its native Jamaica. The Aztecs saw its sweet applications, using it to spice chocolate. Allspice can be purchased whole or ground and is used in both forms. The whole berries, which don't have much fragrance until crushed, will retain their flavor longer.

ANCHO CHILE

A common poblano chile is transformed into an ancho chile through drying, which intensifies the complex fruitiness of the chile. Wrinkled, deep reddish-brown ancho chile peppers also have a mild heat and a slight sweetness. The chile is a staple of savory Mexican cuisines, but its undertones of deep fruit flavors like plum, prune, and raisin also match well with chocolate and coffee. Although ancho chile peppers are dried, they shouldn't be crisp or brittle. Look for a pepper that is still pliable.

ANISESEED

Aniseseed is one of several unrelated spices that add the distinctive flavor of licorice to desserts. The small grayish-green aniseseeds are harvested from an annual herb in the parsley family native to the Middle East and grown widely throughout the Mediterranean. They have a sweet but not overpowering licorice flavor. Aniseseeds are best purchased whole, and they are often toasted before using to unlock their fragrance.

BAY LEAF

Bay is complex. It can taste cinnamony, minty, lemony, peppery, tea-like, or herbaceous. The flavor of bay depends on its cooking method, its companion ingredients, and its quality. Even when a recipe calls for dried bay leaves—the dried leaves are often of a different variety than those available fresh—it's important to use the freshest dried bay leaves you can find. The leaves should be fragrant. Bay leaves don't break down in the cooking process, so you must remove them before serving, but their hard-to-pin-down flavor will remain.

BLACK PEPPER

Black pepper is one of the world's most frequently used spices. Native to South Asia and grown widely in tropical regions around the world, peppercorns are the fruits of a flowering vine. Black peppercorns are produced by cooking immature fruits briefly before drying them. Wrinkled and deep brown or black in color, black peppercorns have a pungent flavor and aroma. The exact flavor profile can vary significantly from bright to hot, with notes of citrus, earth, smoke, or flowers, depending on the spice's origin. It's best to buy whole black peppercorns—look for a consistent, deep color—and grind them as needed.

CANDIED VIOLET

The edible, heart-shaped petals of the violet have a subtle floral and sweet flavor. The fresh petals are often used in salad, and candied petals are a popular addition to sweets throughout Europe.

CARAWAY

Another spice that imparts a whisper of licorice flavor, crescent-moon-shaped caraway has a sharp aroma and earthy, green, and slightly citrusy taste. Caraway, which is botanically related to dill and fennel, is grown widely, but the brownish-green fruit—often incorrectly called a seed—is typically associated with German foods, where it is paired with cabbage and potatoes and baked into breads such as rye bread. It provides a savory balance in sweet baked goods.

CARDAMOM

Green cardamom—as opposed to harder-to-find, bolder, smoke-dried black cardamom—imparts a delicate, bright, and lingering floral sweetness to both sweet and savory dishes. The light green outer pod of the "queen of spices" hides its small, oily, brown-black seeds. Both the pod and the seeds are commonly used in Indian and other Southeast Asian cuisines, as well as in Scandinavian sweets and North African spice mixes. Ground cardamom can be made from the whole pod, including the seeds, or from the seeds alone; if it has a dull brown color, whole cardamom pods have been used. A gray-black color means it was made only with the flavorful seeds.

CAYENNE

The bright-red cayenne pepper is dried and ground to create the powdered form most frequently used in cooking. It is a relatively powerful pepper—typically measuring 30,000 to 50,000 units on the Scoville scale, which measures a pepper's heat, or the amount of capsaicin in the pepper. Ground cayenne is used in small amounts to add heat or to enhance other spices in the dish. Its pungent flavor intensifies as a dish rests.

CHAMOMILE

Chamomile is familiar to many as a calming tea with a delicate floral aroma and a slightly apple-like taste. When used in desserts, this pretty herb is subtle, enhancing other flavors without announcing its presence. Choose a high-quality chamomile for the best results. Chamomile can become bitter if it is oversteeped.

CHINESE FIVE SPICE POWDER

Chinese five spice powder is a variable blend of warm and complex spices, typically star anise, cloves, cinnamon, Szechuan peppercorns, ginger, and fennel seeds, and is commonly used in Chinese cooking to season meats. In combination, the spices act differently than all the same spices added separately to the recipe. Some spice shops create their own version from freshly ground spices.

CHIPOTLE POWDER

Rich and smoky chipotle gets its start as a jalepeño chile that is ripened past its usual immature green state to a ripe, deep red. The jalepeño is then smoke-dried, giving it the distinctive chipotle flavor. Chipotles, which are produced mainly in Mexico, can be used whole or ground to add mild heat (3,000 to 10,000 on the Scoville scale) and depth to dishes.

CINNAMON

There are two different spices sold as "cinnamon": true cinnamon and cassia. They look similar but have distinct flavors that can vary by region, though the spices' origins are not always labeled. *Ceylon*, or Sri Lankan, cinnamon (true cinnamon) is commonly used in Europe and Mexico. It doesn't have the bite most American bakers associate with cinnamon. Instead, its subtle flavor is floral with notes of citrus. *Vietnamese*, or Saigon, cinnamon (cassia) has a pungent, warmer, and slightly bitter flavor that is very popular in Western cuisines. Because of its high oil content, Vietnamese cinnamon is the strongest and richest ground cinnamon and is preferred by bakers. In this book, *cinnamon stick* refers to a thick-barked stick of cassia. Vietnamese and Indonesian cinnamon sticks may be difficult to find. Unlabeled, commonly available cinnamon sticks are most likely Chinese in origin and are a fine choice for baking.

CLOVE

The name *cloves* comes from the Latin *clavus*, or nail, a description of the spice's shape. The unopened flower buds of a tropical evergreen tree, cloves have a rounded head and woody stem. Native to Indonesia, cloves have been used in cooking since at least the sixth century. They are prized for their pungent, spicy flavor and aroma, but if you use too much their flavor can become medicinal.

CORIANDER

Coriander is the tan, spherical fruit—often called a seed—of the cilantro plant, but the spice and the herb taste completely different. Coriander has a bright citrus flavor and intensely floral aroma. Toasting the spice brings out nutty notes. A versatile spice, coriander is popular around the world, especially in India. The spice's essential oils are highly volatile, so whole coriander is preferable to ground.

CUBEB PEPPER

Wrinkled cubeb berries—or "tailed pepper," for their tiny gray-black stalks—have that tingle associated with black pepper plus a deeper flavor similar to allspice and clove and a minty, piney aroma. This spice, grown primarily in Indonesia, might remind you of gin, in which cubeb is often used.

CUMIN

Curved cumin—the seed of the flowering zeera plant, a relative of parsley—has a warm, earthy aroma and pleasingly pungent smoky flavor that has been used in cuisines from India to North Africa to Mexico for millennia. Khaki-colored white cumin is most common; rarer black cumin has a dark brown color and a sweeter and more astringent flavor. Cumin can be used whole or ground.

EARL GREY TEA

Earl Grey tea is black tea blended with oil extracted from the rind of tart bergamot oranges. This fragrant fruit from the Mediterranean is the size of an orange and the color of a lemon, with a flavor that is an unexpectedly delicious marriage of the two. The aroma is elusive—it's a favorite of perfume makers. Since the nineteenth century, Earl Grey tea has been a fixture of teatime in Britain; it works just as well as an ingredient in teatime sweets as it does sipped alongside them.

ELDERFLOWER

The elder plant's blue-black berries (which should be cooked before eating) are rich and winey, but its snowy-white flowers have a soft, sweet, and fruity flavor. The tiny flowers grow in lacy clusters and are best picked soon after they bloom. Once used primarily as a home remedy for all sorts of ills, elderflowers are now prized for the taste they impart to infused syrups and alcohols.

ESPRESSO POWDER

Espresso powder is not designed for making espresso. The finely ground powder, made by brewing espresso and dehydrating it, is designed for bakers. Intensely dark, the powder dissolves quickly in water. It can be used to give a strong but smooth, balanced coffee flavor without the acidity. It also pairs particularly well with chocolate, enhancing the chocolate's flavor without announcing its presence.

FENNEL POLLEN

Like fennel seeds, yellow-hued fennel pollen comes from the fennel plant. To make the spice, both the pollen and a portion of the fennel flower are ground into a fine, fragrant powder. Fennel pollen is a brighter, more intense version of fennel seeds, with a sweeter flavor including hints of citrus. The powerful pollen, produced mainly in Italy and California, can be expensive, but it is typically used sparingly as a finishing spice.

FENNEL SEED

As their name implies, grassy, licorice-flavored fennel seeds also come from the fennel plant. After the plant flowers, the small, curved seeds are dried in the shade to preserve their yellow-green color and refreshing, sweet flavor. Fennel seeds are used in a wide variety of cuisines. In Indian and Asian cooking, the seeds are often roasted to intensify their sweetness. When buying whole fennel seeds, look for seeds with a greenish hue.

FENUGREEK

The fenugreek plant, a member of the pea family, produces hard, golden-brown seeds that look like small pebbles. Native to western Asia and southern Europe, fenugreek seeds have a pungent, assertive aroma and a bitter flavor. When cooked, the spice sweetens and develops flavors similar to maple syrup. (In fact, fenugreek is often used as a flavoring in artificial maple syrup.) Because the flavor of ground fenugreek can fade quickly, purchase it in small amounts.

FLEUR DE SEL

Unlike every other spice or flavor enhancer in this book, fleur de sel does not come from a plant. Like all salts, it is a mineral—but salt is one of the world's oldest seasonings. The flavor of salts can vary dramatically depending on the concentration and types of other minerals present besides sodium chloride. Different types of salt—and different methods of harvesting—also have different textures. Fleur de sel, harvested from salt-evaporation ponds in France, is a slightly sweet and floral salt prized for its assertive flavor and crunchy texture.

GINGER

Ginger is the rhizome of a leafy tropical plant. Under a scaly beige skin, ginger's fibrous, pale yellow flesh has a pungent scent and a fresh, spicy taste. (Heat and pungency are dependent on the variety of ginger and when it was harvested.) Fresh ginger can add a bright, almost floral heat to a dish; look for firm, plump fresh ginger. Dried, ground ginger doesn't have the same intensity as fresh, but it has its own admirable attributes, adding richness and spiciness to dishes. Look for a fine, not fibrous, ground ginger with a pungent but not harsh aroma.

HIBISCUS

Beautiful, vibrantly colored hibiscus flowers grow in warm climates around the globe. Dried, the flower is widely used in making both hot and cold beverages with a deep burgundy color and a refreshingly tangy, lemony tart, slightly earthy flavor.

JASMINE GREEN TEA

Star-shaped jasmine flowers grow in the same climate as China's best known teas, and have long been used to scent the naturally absorbent tea leaves. Traditionally, green tea is mixed with just-bloomed jasmine flowers to absorb their aroma, a process that may be repeated for higher-quality teas. The jasmine gives the tea a subtle floral aroma and sweet taste.

JUNIPER

Blue-black juniper berries smell immediately of gin, which gets its flavor from the pungent berries—more properly, cones—of a cold-climate evergreen tree. Juniper grows abundantly in the Alpine region, and its berries are common in European cuisines. The delicate berries are picked by hand to avoid damaging them and are most often dried before use. Look for dried berries that are still supple. The dried berries have a piney and slightly citrusy aroma and add a fresh flavor to foods. The volatile oils in juniper dissipate quickly, so the berries should be ground just before use.

KAFFIR LIME LEAF

The makrut lime tree is native to Southeast Asia, and its unusual double leaves are often used in Thai and Balinese cuisines. When cut, the dark green leaves, most commonly called kaffir lime leaves, smell of citrus—an unexpected combination of orange, lemon, and lime—and the taste is similar to the floral, zingy taste of citrus zest but without the acidity. Leathery, fresh leaves can be found in the produce section of Asian markets. Dried leaves are also available; look for crisp, green dried leaves.

LAVENDER

Floral and slightly citrusy lavender, which grows in temperate climates around the world, is a member of the mint family, and like its kin—basil, rosemary, and thyme, to name just a few—the plant has been at home in the kitchen for centuries. The flowers, picked just at bloom, are most commonly used in cooking, but the stems are also edible. The more fragrant the flower, the better its flavor. (But if it smells of piney camphor, it will also taste that way.) Be sure to buy food-grade lavender.

LEMONGRASS

Lemongrass is just what its name describes: a citrus-flavored grass. Native to India and common in Southeast Asian cooking, lemongrass has recently become popular in Western dishes—and easier to find in grocery stores. The herb's lemon-like aroma and flavor (minus lemon's sourness) are most concentrated in the pale stalk of the grass. Look for fragrant, moist stalks, and peel off the tough outer leaves before using. The flavor can be released by bashing the stalk with a mallet or anything heavy; its flavor will intensify with long cooking.

LEMON VERBENA

Native to South America, lemon verbena is a pretty and impossibly fragrant tree. The pale-green pointed leaves smell of pure lemon and taste of lemon, too, minus the acidity. Fresh lemon verbena can be difficult to find, but it is worth hunting for. Try the produce section of a well-stocked grocery store or your local farmers' market.

MACE

Mace and nutmeg come from the same evergreen tree native to Indonesia. When nutmeg is harvested and shelled, a bright-red, lacy covering is removed from the seed. When that webbing, known as an aril, is dried to a light brown color, it is mace. One of the less common spices, mace has similarities to warming nutmeg but is lighter and more subtle in flavor, with notes of citrus and a floral aroma. Mace is sold whole—a piece of mace is called a "blade"—or ground.

MAHLAB

Made from the seeds inside the pits of sour St. Lucie cherries, mahlab has a complicated flavor, tasting at once of almonds, citrus, and vanilla—it's a spice box contained in one tiny seed. (Add too much, though, and mahlab's pleasantly bitter notes can easily overwhelm a recipe.) Buy whole seeds and grind them yourself—that's the best option—or you can buy it already ground. Once ground, mahlab turns rancid quickly, so buy it from a store that you know is rotating its stock often.

MATCHA

A finely ground, vibrantly green tea, matcha is central to the ritual Japanese tea ceremony, which dates back a thousand years. More recently, the vegetal tea has become a popular ingredient in cooking. The powder—produced by finely milling tea leaves that have been grown in the shade—adds a sweet and slightly bitter flavor and can also be used to color foods a pleasant shade of green.

NIGELLA

A small, hard, sharp-cornered, coal-black seed, nigella doesn't have much of an aroma, but it has a memorably nutty, smoky flavor. The spice, native to western Asia, is often used in bread baking in Eastern European, Middle Eastern, and Indian cuisines. Although it is sometimes called "black cumin," nigella isn't related to that spice. Nigella is sold whole; look for whole seeds with no bits of flaky husk.

NUTMEG

Native to the Banda Islands of Indonesia, nutmeg is a pungent, warm, and slightly sharp spice. It is the hard, almost-wooden seed of an apricot-like fruit that also produces mace. Because the volatile oils of the dried nutmeg can dissipate quickly, it is best to buy whole nutmeg. Look for whole nutmeg with some oiliness and without insect holes. Grate whole nutmeg for your recipes; the results will be entirely different—and far superior—than if you use ground nutmeg.

PAPRIKA

The flavor and aroma of paprika—a bright-red powder made from a fruit related to traditional chile peppers—depends on the ratio of dried flesh to seeds and veins and on the drying and curing method. A higher ratio of seeds, for instance, can produce a more bitter paprika, and the milling process, which generates heat, can introduce a caramelized flavor or a sharp and bitter one. The majority of paprika comes from Hungary and Spain and is typically marked as sweet, mild, or hot. It can be used to give foods a striking red color as well as the fruitiness associated with chiles without the intensity of their heat.

PIMENTÓN DE LA VERA/SMOKED PAPRIKA

 Pimentón de la Vera is a type of smoked paprika harvested near the rainy Tietar River in La Vera, Spain. Smoked paprika is made from the same fruits as paprika, slow-dried in a smokehouse and ground to a silky texture. Pimentón de la Vera is only smoked over oak-wood, giving it a memorable intensity and deep savory notes.

PINK PEPPERCORN

 Dried pink peppercorns come from a different plant than black and white peppercorns. The schinus tree, native to Peru, pro-duces these pink berries with a hard brown seed inside. The pink portion has little flavor or aroma, but when crushed, the seed inside gives off an aroma similar to black peppercorns and has a warm, bright, and astringent flavor. (Soft, brined pink peppercorns may come from the traditional pepper vine or the schinus tree.)

POPPY SEED

 Tiny poppy seeds burst by the hundreds from the woody capsules that form after a poppy plant has flowered. The most com-mon types of poppy seeds are white poppy seeds, which have a sweet aroma and lightly nutty flavor, and blue poppy seeds, which are really a dull gray and have a slightly more assertive flavor. The blue version is more popular in Euro-pean cooking. The oily seeds can become rancid quickly and should be stored in the refrigerator.

ROSE PETALS (DRIED)

 Roses have a distinctive sweet, floral, and slightly musky aroma. Less well known is their light, grassy flavor. Although any scented variety of rose is edible, it is essential to buy food-grade dried rose petals that have not been treated with dangerous pesticides. Rose water, made by steeping fresh petals in water, has the fragrance of rose petals with slightly piney, floral flavors. (Don't mistake rose water and rose syrup; the latter is very sweet.) Different brands of rose water have different intensities, so initially add less than the recipe calls for and taste before adding more.

ROSEMARY

 Native to the Mediterra-nean, where it thrives in sandy soil, fresh rosemary has a woody stem and needle-like leaves with a memorable piney and minty aroma and a slightly citrusy, warm flavor. Fresh rosemary can be found in the supermarket produce section. The herb is espe-cially popular in Italian cooking.

SAFFRON

Saffron is the dried bright-red stigmas of the saffron crocus. Saffron has an earthy, bittersweet flavor and a hay-like aroma, and it stains foods a distinctive sunny yellow. The coveted spice is one of the most expensive in the world, due to its labor-intensive harvesting process. Saffron crocuses are gathered by hand during a three-week fall harvest, and a mere three stigmas are extracted from each flower. The stigmas are then dried to form saffron threads. Because of its cost, saffron is often adulterated; buy it from a reputable source. "Coupe"-grade Spanish saffron is the highest-quality widely available saffron and has a strong, concentrated flavor. Iranian and Kashmiri saffron are also in this category but are more difficult to find.

SESAME SEEDS (BLACK)

With leaves that give off an unpleasant smell, the sesame plant is not enticing. Its seeds, however, are very popular in Middle Eastern, Asian, and North American cooking. The tiny, tear-shaped seeds come in many varieties. Black sesame seeds, which are unhulled, have an assertive, nutty flavor and add a different flavor and texture than the tan-colored sesame seeds frequently sold as "unhulled." Because of their high oil content, sesame seeds can turn rancid quickly.

SESAME SEEDS (UNHULLED)

These tan, tear-shaped seeds are the dried seeds of the sesame plant. Sesame seeds come in many varieties, including black. The tan sesame seeds, known as "unhulled," have a subtle buttery, nutty flavor and add crunch to baked goods. When hulled, these seeds are white and lack some of the crunch of the unhulled version. Don't confuse their brownish color with that of toasted sesame seeds, which have a more pronounced flavor. Because of their high oil content, sesame seeds can turn rancid quickly.

STAR ANISE

Star anise gets its name from its elegant and distinctive eight-pointed shape and its potent, lingering aniseed-like flavor with a hint of warm spice (although it is actually unrelated to licorice-scented aniseed). This pretty fruit of a small Asian evergreen tree is picked unripe and green and dried to a deep reddish-brown. Star anise is popular in Chinese cuisine, and it is a key ingredient in Chinese five spice powder. The spice is used whole—the star-shaped pericarp is the main source of the flavor, and the seeds inside the pericarp are mild and slightly nutty—or can be ground.

SUMAC

Sumacs grow wild across North America and the Mediterranean, but only 6 of the more than 150 varieties of the rhus tree produce the edible sumac fruit, which is brick red and pleasantly tart with a fruity aroma. Sumac spice is sold ground: the ripe, hairy berries of these sumac trees are handpicked and dried and then pulverized. Salt is added as a preservative. Look for deeply colored sumac, which means it has more flesh than seeds and stems, and a slightly oily, uniformly coarse texture. Sumac is used throughout the Middle East, playing the same souring role that lemon or vinegar does in other dishes, and is an ingredient in za'atar.

TAMARIND

Tamarind is harvested from the fruit pods of the large tamarind tree, native to East Africa and grown in tropical climates around the world. The brittle-shelled pods are broken to reveal brown, sticky tamarind pulp threaded with tough fibers and dotted with shiny black seeds. The pulp is valued for its tangy, slightly citrusy flavor with earthy undertones. Tamarind can be purchased as a concentrate or paste, but it is best straight from the fresh tamarind pods, which are sometimes available at Asian, Indian, Caribbean, and Latin American markets or in a well-stocked grocery store's produce section.

THYME

Thyme is a versatile herb common throughout Europe, the United States, and the Middle East. The small, gray-green leaves of a bushy shrub, thyme has a pungent, warm, and slightly spicy flavor and aroma. It is sold both fresh and dried. Fresh thyme, which is found in the supermarket produce section, has a milder, brighter flavor than the strong, earthier, and slightly smoky dried version. Dried thyme is an ingredient in za'atar.

TURMERIC

Indigenous to Southeast Asia, deep-yellow turmeric is the rhizome of a tropical plant that belongs to the ginger family. Fresh turmeric is sweet, mild, and aromatic; the more common dried turmeric is earthier and slightly bitter. The drying process includes boiling the rhizome, which hardens it and makes it difficult to grind without specialized equipment, so dried turmeric must be purchased ground. Turmeric is often used primarily for its color; it can easily stain anything it comes in contact with.

URFA BIBER

Urfa biber, from the Urfa region of southeastern Turkey, is a deeply purple chile with a unique taste that is at once rich, fruity, and hot. Urfa biber is often described as tasting like raisins and coffee, and its heat is deceptive. At first taste it can be mild, but that mellow heat builds. Urfa biber is typically sold ground into flakes. It should be vibrantly colored and retain some moisture from the pepper's high oil content.

VANILLA BEAN

The vanilla bean is the long seed pod of an orchid native to Central America. Vanilla is difficult to grow, requiring hand pollination, and curing vanilla beans is a time-consuming and labor-intensive process. The tasteless green pods are cured and fermented to create the familiar shriveled and fragrant vanilla beans. There are four main types of vanilla: sweet and spicy Mexican, full-bodied and creamy Bourbon, deeply vanilla Indonesian, and floral Tahitian. With any variety, look for dark, supple, and aromatic pods.

WHITE PEPPER

White peppercorns come from the same fruit as black peppercorns. To produce white peppercorns, the outer portion—or pericarp—of the peppercorn is removed, either mechanically or by soaking and macerating the fruits, which are picked early in the ripening process. The fruits are then dried in the sun, but without the enzymes found in the pericarp, the peppercorns do not blacken during the drying process. White pepper is subtler than black, providing heat without dominating a dish.

ZA'ATAR

The word *za'atar* is sometimes used in the Middle East to describe thyme or marjoram, but it most often refers to a complex blend of herbaceous thyme, toasted sesame seeds, tart sumac, and salt. The combination—which varies somewhat by region and spice maker—is tangy and earthy. It is commonly used in Middle Eastern cooking, baked into or sprinkled on breads or used to season meats.

Resources

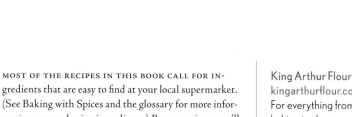

MOST OF THE RECIPES IN THIS BOOK CALL FOR IN-gredients that are easy to find at your local supermarket. (See Baking with Spices and the glossary for more information on purchasing ingredients.) But sometimes you'll want to seek out a particular brand or an unusual spice. These are the places I turn to for those ingredients.

Amazon.com
For fresh kaffir lime leaves and Valrhona Dutch-process cocoa powder

Bazzininuts.com
For nuts and dried figs

Bob's Red Mill
bobsredmill.com
For fine semolina, buckwheat flour, oat flour, and tapioca flour

The Chef's Garden
chefs-garden.com
For herbs (including lemon verbena)

Guittard Chocolate Company
guittard.com
For chocolate and cocoa powder

India Tree
indiatree.com
For light and dark muscovado sugar and sanding sugar

JB Prince
jbprince.com
For baking tools such as baking trays, rolling pins, and ice cream scoops

Kalustyan's
kalustyans.com
For spices (including mahlab), extracts, and candied violets

King Arthur Flour
kingarthurflour.com
For everything from flour and Dutch-process cocoa to baking tools

Le Sanctuaire
lesanctuaire.com
For spices and vanilla beans

Nielsen-Massey
nielsenmassey.com
For vanilla extract, vanilla beans, rose water, and orange blossom water

Nuts.com
For nuts, dried persimmon, and candied orange peel

N.Y. Cake
nycake.com
For chocolate and baking tools such as baking trays

Penzeys Spices
penzeys.com
For spices

The Spice House
spicehouse.com
For spices

Whole Foods Market
Multiple locations across the United States, Canada, and the United Kingdom:
find locations at wholefoodsmarket.com
For date sugar, coconut palm sugar, freeze-dried berries, coconut flakes, evaporated goat's milk, and other specialty items and spices

Ziyad
ziyad.com
For rose water

Acknowledgments

FIRST AND FOREMOST, A BIG THANK-YOU TO MY three boys, the loves of my life, for your patience with me during the long hours of recipe testing at home throughout the day and weekends. There is no job more fulfilling or gratifying than being your mother.

To my two mothers, Amma and Teresa, who help and support me in everything I do and every dream that I pursue. Without you both, this would not be possible. Your support is everything.

To my loving sister, Jehan, for your unwavering support, encouragement, and love. I love you so much.

To my other babies, my lucky five, for all your questions and enthusiasm about this book and for being my consistent recipe testers. I adore you.

To my agent, Coleen O'Shea, for your loyalty and diligence every step of the way. I relish our frequent morning chats filled with laughter. You are a gem. I can't wait to do this with you all over again.

To my writer, April White, for your patience and amazing ability to put my jumbled thoughts into clear, coherent, and magical words.

To my photographer Vanessa Rees, for making everything look so delectable.

To Jane Katte and Lauren La Penna, for your fantastic help with this book—and then some.

To Rochelle Bourgault, Nicole McConville, Julia Gaviria, and the whole team at Roost Books who made this book a reality.

To my friend and mentor Sherry Yard for encouraging and supporting me to pursue my dreams. For being my fan but also my fiercest critic. Your insight is invaluable. You always push me to be my very best. You are my guiding voice.

To Ibby and my loved ones on Private Road, who are more than friends. My extended family. Your constant love, enthusiasm, and support mean a great deal to me. Our meals together nourish my heart and my soul.

To my darling Meme for always being my constant, my true fan, and loving "J mother." You are the one friend I know I can always count on when I need one. I love you.

To my brilliant and ambitious Sana, for our long walks, our priceless time together, and our "power talks." Thank you for answering every call, listening to every complaint, and loving me unconditionally.

To my Khala, my support, my friend Rubab. Somehow, somewhere our souls danced together. Our love and understanding are some of the great joys in my life. I can never thank you enough for being there, being you, and being mine.

To Danielle, my friend who sees the light in everything. Thank you for sticking with me all these years and being such a great cheerleader.

To my lovely Pat for pointing me ten years ago in a direction that I wanted before I knew myself. I miss you.

To my friend Karsha, for telling me to envision myself living my dreams.

And last but not least, to my most favorite person, my abbu, for believing in me before I ever believed in myself. There are no words to convey how much you are missed. My memories with you live on in this book, in this labor of love.

Index

About the Author

MALIKA AMEEN IS A CLASSICALLY TRAINED pastry chef whose South Asian heritage sparked her love of spices—sweet and savory—in desserts. Her cooking journey has taken her from the East Coast to the West Coast and back to her home in the Midwest. As pastry chef at the legendary hotel Chateau Marmont in Los Angeles, she earned accolades for desserts like her walnut cardamom snowball cookies and her sticky toffee pudding, which she brought with her to her hometown of Chicago, where she opened the acclaimed restaurant Aigre Doux. Malika starred on Bravo's *Top Chef: Just Desserts* and frequently appears on local and national television. She is currently a culinary consultant and custom-order pastry chef. She lives in Chicago with her children.